EVALUATION
OF RECREATION
AND PARK
PROGRAMS

EVALUATION OF RECREATION AND PARK PROGRAMS

WILLIAM F. THEOBALD

Chairman, Recreation Studies Program
Purdue University, West Lafayette, Indiana

JOHN WILEY & SONS
New York   Chichester   Brisbane   Toronto

Library of Congress Cataloging in Publication Data:

Theobald, William F
  Evaluation of recreation and park programs.

  Bibliography:p.
  Includes index.
  1. Recreational research—Methodology. I. Title.
GV181.46.T47   790'.07'2   78-24227
ISBN 0-471-01797-3

Printed in the United States of America

10 9 8 7 6 5 4 3 2 1

To
Sharon, Gregg, and Amanda

PREFACE

Decision makers responsible for policy, planning, and coordination in leisure services need better, more definitive information available to make intelligent choices among competing program alternatives.

Increased public demand for leisure programs, coupled with shrinking dollar allocations for services, often affect administrative program decisions. How can recreators determine which programs warrant continuation or increased expenditures? Which programs should be cut back or eliminated altogether? These choices place a heavy responsibility upon program personnel who often rely on instinct or other nonempirical data to make program decisions. There is a growing need for trained program evaluators, but the supply, especially in leisure services, falls far short of the demand. Both the lack of provision for and the lack of knowledge of evaluation techniques are serious liabilities when practitioners try to justify the effectiveness of recreation programs.

Evaluation of Recreation and Park Programs synthesizes the approaches to problems in designing and conducting evaluation research in the leisure-service field. The two main purposes of this book are: (1) to describe in one volume the current literature, methodology, and research on recreation program evaluation that can only be found in a potpourri of documents and reports, and (2) to identify serious weaknesses in the literature and to provide viable alternatives to program assessment. This book includes conceptual frameworks proposed in recreation program evaluation and offers practical techniques for conducting evaluation studies.

While this book primarily serves as an introduction to evaluation for university and college students, it can also serve as a basic or supplemental text for recreation education, program, or administration courses where students are taught how to assess the effectiveness of leisure-service programs. It may be used as a definitive reference for recreation practitioners, graduate students, and advanced undergraduates engaged in the evaluation of recreation programs at any level.

The book is intended to enable the reader to conceptualize the goals and rationale for ongoing recreation programs and the methods of defining behavioral and program objectives that are clear, specific, and measurable. Furthermore, it provides a readable, nonmathematical introduction to evaluation research, the variety of methods employed to obtain information, and how to interpret results and make conclusions and recommendations.

I am indebted to many people for the contents of this book, especially to those who are mentioned below.

Professor Richard G. Kraus of Temple University for his guidance, writings, teaching, and support. He provided the intellectual stimulation and academic foundations.

Dr. Elliott M. Avedon of the University of Waterloo for sharing his colleagueship and friendship during trying times, and providing his understanding of the real meaning of leisure and culture.

Wayne Anderson and Andrew Ford of John Wiley & Sons for their support and encouragement.

Dr. Allen Sapora of the University of Illinois and Dr. Tony Mobley of Indiana University for their constructive criticisms and reviews.

My colleagues, students, and friends at Purdue University, the University of Waterloo, and Brooklyn College who afforded the opportunities for personal and professional growth.

Elfie Barnett at the University of Waterloo and Dianne Renner at Purdue University for their expert skills in helping to prepare the manuscript.

My wife Sharon whose alert mind entered into many fruitful discussions, and whose understanding came from her own creativity as a teacher and artist.

William F. Theobald

CONTENTS

Evaluation Models   91
Examples of Goal-Attainment Models   93
Examples of Systems Models   96
Additional Evaluation Approaches   99
Summary   102
References   103

6 **Design of Evaluation Research**   **105**
Analysis of Program Effectiveness   105
Conceptualizing Goals and Objectives   107
Objectives in Recreation Program Evaluation   108
General Versus Specific Objectives   109
Formulating the Questions   117
Measurement   117
The Program Sequence   119
Sources of Recreation and Park Data   120
Data-Gathering Techniques   121
Experimental Versus Nonexperimental Research   123
Summary   125
References   125

7 **Measurement in Evaluation Research**   **127**
Choosing the Appropriate Measurement Tools   127
Secondary Analysis   133
Measurement Variables   133
Reliability and Validity   138
Measuring Program Effects   140
Effects of Evaluation   141
Contemporary Evaluation Models   145
The Recreation Program Evaluation Process   152
Summary   158
References   159

PART THREE   **THE PRODUCT OF EVALUATION IN RECREATION
             AND PARKS**

8 **Results of Evaluation Research**   **163**
Performance Measures   163
Writing the Evaluation Report   164
Communicating the Results of Evaluation   167
Utilizing Evaluation Recommendations   167
Choices of Recommendations   171
Conclusion   174
Summary   176
References   177

Appendix   **179**

Bibliography   **189**

Index   **199**

EVALUATION OF RECREATION AND PARK PROGRAMS

PART ONE

THE PLAN FOR EVALUATION IN RECREATION AND PARKS

1

THE NEED FOR
EVALUATION

Since the early 1960s, the federal governments of North America have embarked upon a course to substantially increase funding levels to a number of interdisciplinary programs related to the leisure service fields. A plethora of creative and innovative social action and economic development programs were begun—such as the War on Poverty, Opportunities for Youth, Local Initiative Programs, Neighborhood Youth Corps, and other demonstration projects—to enhance the quality of life for the nations' poor and impoverished. Provinces, states, and cities followed the federal initiative and began their own programs to alleviate regional and local problems. These programs made funds available to provide diverse opportunities for leisure, such as acquiring additional amounts of recreational space, building senior citizen and neighborhood centers, beautifying and improving the urban environment, and providing jobs in recreation and parks for the under- and unemployed.

It is estimated that the leisure industry in North America amounts to almost $175 billion per year, and of this amount, government spends in excess of 5.5½ billion dollars annually on outdoor recreation alone.[1]

> Never in history have leisure and recreation attained the status they enjoy in the U.S. today . . . Year after year, Americans are spending more time and money on leisure activities than any other people . . . Other countries, too, are beginning to get rapid growth in recreation. In fact, World Leisure and Recreation Association, a United Nations affiliate, is studying how to help nations cope with their problems.[2]

However, a number of actions in the 1970s have reduced or virtually eliminated expenditures for many of these government programs. One reason for this action was that the programs failed to achieve their desired objectives. A major difficulty was a lack of clear, specific, and measurable program objectives. It is doubtful, however, that decisions were based upon evaluation methodology as it has emerged today. Consequently, at the federal level, most programs now insist on accountability, and demand evaluation of program outcomes, and require that a proportion of operating funds be budgeted to determine program effectiveness.

At the local level, all municipal departments, whether recreation, education, health, or safety, are required to prove their legitimacy and effectiveness in order to justify continued community support. In general, there tends to be a delicate balance between faith and fact, which may be indicative of citizens' views of authority and its institutions, as opposed to their scepticisms and needs for assurance of worth. Both the demand for and the evidence required for community support depends in large measure on the nature of the relationship between government agencies and the public.

Governments today are being pressured to justify an activity in relation to its costs. To know whether a program or activity is worthwhile indicates that the public believes many social problems can be overcome by planned intervention. This strategy, whether it is applied to leisure, education, or transportation, can be based upon existing knowledge, including the design of better solutions through continued research. Planned social change is apparent on the national scene, as evidenced by current approaches to such problems as hunger, lack of adequate housing, and unemployment. These unsolved problems pose a serious liability for those administrators who are responsible for making program decisions. Allen Sapora suggests it is the recreation and park profession who must face this challenge and without the development and utilization of scientific evaluation methodology, it faces an uncertain future:

> *Administrators of recreation and parks can be described as operating on the "crises principle," with new crises to contend with nearly every day. The current explosive development in the field has put so much pressure on all of us that little energy and few resources are left to evaluate the results of operations and to determine in what directions we should proceed.*[3]

Increased public demand for leisure programs, coupled with shrinking dollar allocations because of inflation and other economic factors often force recreation administrators to make crucial program decisions. On what defensible basis can recreators determine which programs warrant continuation or increased expenditures? Which programs should be cut back or eliminated altogether? Meserow, Pompel, and Reich indicate that it is an illusion to continue to provide municipal recreation programs without providing for a substantial appraisal component:

> *REALIZING IT IS ONE THING to provide a park or recreation service*

and quite another to assess its true effectiveness, many administra-
tors are presently seeking new methods of evaluation which will
indicate just how efficiently the taxpayers' dollars are being ex-
pended. Probably the most elusive element in this search is a system
with which evidence of effectiveness can be gathered and analyzed. [4]

David De Shane, reacting to the current state of evaluation in public
recreation programs, likewise suggests:

Most programs continue to function only because we have resorted
to "head counting" to justify their existence. Even then, the stand-
ards of required attendance are set so low that considering the
percentage of potential users we fail to reach a significant number
of citizens. Few communities have attempted, or dared, to venture
beyond this stage in evaluating the quality of any recreation program
or in measuring its impact on people. This kind of research is still
"pie in the sky" to many people in the profession. If we continue
to ignore the need and potential of practical research our service to
people will of necessity become less and less meaningful. [5]

The lack of provision for or knowledge of evaluation techniques hind-
ers any attempts to justify the effectiveness of recreation programs.
The growing need for trained leisure service program evaluators, falls
far short of the supply. Only a handful of colleges and universities
offer a course on recreation program evaluation. This fact is in sharp
contrast to those many institutions that conduct program development
courses. Recreation practitioners and educators agree on the importance of evaluation, but in fact few of them devote but cursory attention to it.

Taxpayers are concerned about the cost and effectiveness of government services, especially at the local or municipal levels. Complaints often take the form of specific questions such as "What's wrong
with our recreation and park department?" Although this complaint
may be well intended, many recreation administrators see it as a threat
to them or their profession, and immediately become defensive about
the program. For example, a parent who had complained to a recreation and park director that her daughter was trampled during an
Easter Egg Hunt was given a discourse on the philosophy of special
programs. In the past, those questioning the system and those de-
fending it attempted to debate its merits on a theoretical basis. All too
often, the debate bogged down into a battle of words and a show of
emotions. McLean and Spears ask the question, "HOW ARE LEISURE
SERVICES measured and evaluated? [They answer:] In the past the
success or failure of programs has been judged by the number of
complaints received. If we are truthful we will admit that we have
been flying by the seat of our pants." [6]

Today, concerned individuals approach the problem of leisure service from a different perspective. Often, groups of taxpayers and elected officials who are responsible for funding municipal services require recreation administrators to account more effectively for their expenditures. Those who pay the bills are in effect saying: "Show us that the participants in the recreation program are deriving the desired benefits from the money you are spending." While some recreators may see this attitude as a threat, the accountability requirement should help them provide a recreation program of consistently high quality at the least possible cost.

Charles Pierce suggests that the growth of recreation evaluation has not kept up with the growth of municipal recreation programs. He feels that this delay is necessary in order to "discover causal relationships between our practices and the results of these practices."[7] Recreators who plan programs and make policy and funding decisions must realize that if new knowledge is to find its way into new programs, especially within budgetary restrictions, then current activities must be evaluated to determine future resource allocations. At the same time, new activities must be pretested and evaluated carefully before they become an established part of the program. One technique to pretesting new program activities would be to offer a series of mini courses or activities and test the public's response. For example, a recreation and park department might organize tours to two local artists' studios before officially expanding costs for bus rentals, professional tour guides, and trips to sophisticated urban center studios. Pretesting of new or expanded activities should be an essential element in recreation program development.

As mentioned, recreation and park programs, despite inflation and economic uncertainty, continue to account for a large proportion of governmental expenditures. Although the provision of organized recreation services on the municipal level is a relatively new phenomenon, its growth has been remarkable.

GROWTH OF LEISURE IN CONTEMPORARY CIVILIZATION

The twentieth century can be categorized as a period marked by a substantial growth of leisure for all peoples. Never before in modern history, has there been so much free time, time away from the toils of work. The Industrial Revolution was but a harbinger for what has now become known as "The Leisure Revolution." A number of factors have accounted for the growth of leisure in contemporary civilization.

First, since 1850, the average work week has decreased from approximately 70 to 37½ hours. Although fluctuations in this average occur periodically, there has been almost a constant decline (see Figure 1.1).

A shorter work week, together with longer vacations and more holidays, result in a significant amount of leisure time. Workers retire at an earlier age now than any other time in modern history. Our grandparents retired at age 65, our parents at 55 or 60, and if the trend continues, the present generation can look forward to a life of leisure at approximately age 50.

A second contributing factor to increased leisure time is population increase. The U.S. population today is approximately 216 million; and Canada's 22.5 million people add slightly more than 10 percent Notwithstanding the pill and other population control measures, the rate of increase in the total North American population amounts to almost three million people each year. Children account for one-third of the total, and those individuals under 18 and over 60 years of age are

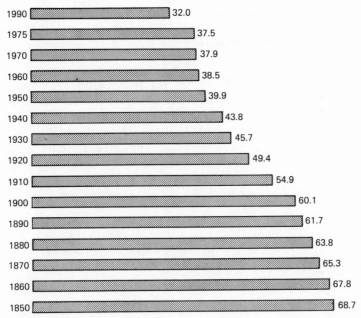

FIGURE 1.1 Average Work Week, 1850–1990, All Industries
SOURCES: de Grazia, Sebastian, *Of Time, Work and Leisure* (New York: Doubleday & Co., 1962), p. 419. U.S. Bureau of the Census, *1976, Facts* (Washington, D.C.: U.S. Government Printing Office, 1977).

[a] Estimate by the Delphi Forecast (Society of Manufacturing Engineers and the University of Michigan), Associated Press Wire Service, July 6, 1978.

quickly increasing groups. Traditionally, these two groups have had more leisure time available to them than any other age group.

Coupled with increasing population is longer life expectancy. Actuarial tables established by major insurance companies clearly demonstrate that people are living longer than ever before in recorded history. Life expectancy for North American women is approximately 75 years, while for men the figure falls to 69 years. Medical science has conquered or controlled many dread diseases that have struck down people of earlier generations. Further medical advancements may increase longevity and thereby add even more to the population increase.

A fourth factor is increased technology. Automated machines have replaced humans in many job situations. Management extolled the speed, dependability, and costs savings of machines. Unions, on the other hand, countered by conducting job actions, which at best only slowed the changeover rate from human to machine. At the present time, another technological development, cybernetics (the utilization of computer memory for control of machine systems) threatens to disrupt the delicate balance between humans and machines. When cybernetics are combined with automation, human operation and control are eliminated. This technological expansion has led to greater amounts of leisure time for many individuals. As Alvin Toffler's *Future Shock* points out:

> *Leisure-time pursuits will become an increasingly important basis for differences between people, as the society itself shifts from a work orientation towards greater involvement in leisure. In the United States, since the turn of the century alone, the society's measurable commitment to work has plummeted by nearly a third. This is a massive deployment of the society's time and energy. As this commitment declines further, we shall advance into an era of breathtaking fun specialism—much of it based on sophisticated technology.*[8]

Concomitant with the increase in available leisure time is a dramatic rise in the acceptance by municipal government of the responsibility for providing recreation and park services.

EXPANSION OF RECREATION AND PARK SERVICES

Three significant developments during the early to mid 1900s influenced the growth and expansion of U.S. public recreation programs.

At the onset of World War I, the Playground and Recreation Association of America (now the National Recreation and Park Association) was asked by the federal government to establish recreation programs adjacent to military bases. Almost 63,000 people, both volunteer and paid staff, were utilized to form municipal recreation programs that provided for the leisure needs of both military persons and civilians. At the conclusion of the war, some who had participated in these extensive recreation programs wanted to continue participation when they returned home. The emphasis was transferred then to those local municipalities who were asked to provide the kinds of recreational opportunities that had occurred during wartime.

In the early 1930s a severe economic depression befell the American nation. Millions of men and women were unemployed, and the total economic climate of the country was desperate. In order to alleviate unemployment and to infuse dollars into the economy, the federal government instituted a program called the Works Progress Administration (WPA). This project was intended to help control unemployment by creating jobs in the public sector. From 1930 to 1935, the WPA and its various programs constructed more recreation and park facilities, both indoor and outdoor, than had been created in the country during the entire history prior to that time. The WPA built community centers, swimming pools, golf courses, stadiums, marinas, and a host of other recreational and cultural facilities that continue to be used today. According to Foster Dulles, "By the close of 1937 some $500,000,000 had been allotted for buildings, 881 new parks, 1,500 athletic fields, 440 swimming pools, 3,500 tennis courts, 123 golf courses, and 28 miles of ski trials."[9] Another federal government program, the Civilian Conservation Corps (CCC) put thousands upon thousands of young people to work creating new parks and enhancing the natural environment throughout the United States.

As in the First World War, World War II saw an immediate mobilization of thousands of young people called into military service on relatively short notice. The federal government, aware of some of the recreational problems that had arisen during the First World War, established special service units within each branch of the military. The function of these units was to provide recreational and cultural programs for military persons who were far from their homes. In addition to the United Service Organization, the American Red Cross and other religious, youth serving and voluntary agencies worked cooperatively in order to help offer recreational programs.

With respect to municipal recreation, Figure 1.2 indicates the growth of local programs between the period 1945–1970. New legislation in a number of states enabled local municipalities to acquire land, construct and maintain facilities, provide leadership, and raise taxes to

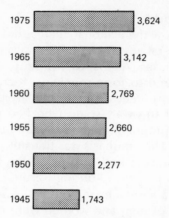

FIGURE 1.2   Number of U.S. Local Agencies Providing Recreation Services
SOURCES: National Recreation and Park Association, *Recreation and Park Yearbooks,
1956, 1961, 1966.*   Henkel, Donald D. and Geoffrey C. Godbey, *Parks, Recreation and
Leisure Services: Employment in the Public Sector: Status and Trends* (Arlington, Va.:
National Recreation and Park Association, 1977).

support recreation programs. Over a 25-year period following the end
of World War II, the number of local agencies that provided recreation
service more than doubled.

With the growth of public agencies providing recreation services,
the number of paid workers in local public recreation and park programs increased correspondingly (see Figure 1.3). These figures represent both the full and part-time personnel responsible for providing
leadership, supervisory and administrative support in municipal rec-

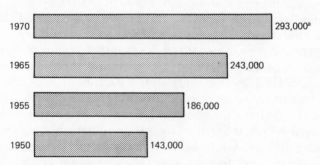

FIGURE 1.3   Number of Paid Workers in Local Recreation Services, 1950–
1970

[a] Estimate.
SOURCE: National Recreation and Park Association, *Recreation and Park Yearbooks,
1956, 1961, 1966.*

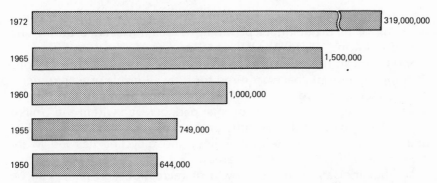

FIGURE 1.4   Total Recreation and Park Acreage in the United States, 1950–
1972
SOURCES: National Recreation and Park Association, *Recreation and Park Yearbooks,
1956, 1961, 1966.*   Bureau of Outdoor Recreation, U.S. Department of the Interior,
Outdoor Recreation: A Legacy for America. (Washington, D.C.: U.S. Government Printing Office, 1973).

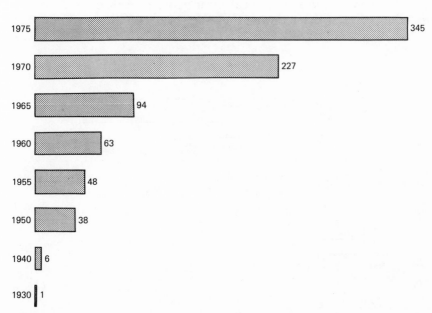

FIGURE 1.5   Number of Recreation and Park Curricula in North American
Colleges and Universities, 1930–1975
SOURCES: Stein, Thomas A. and Roger A. Lancaster. "Professional Preparation," *Parks
and Recreation* **11**:7 (July 1976), p. 58.   Stein, Thomas A., *SPRE Report on the State of
Recreation and Park Education in Canada and the United States* (Arlington, Va.: National
Recreation and Park Association, 1975), p. 4.

reation. Not only did local departments grow, but there was also a doubling of paid personnel providing recreation service during the period following World War II.

Nowhere can the growth of recreation and parks be more obvious than the amount of space acquired for it by all levels of government. As indicated in Figure 1.4, there has been, and continues to be significant increases in the amount of total park acreage within the United States. The growth and popularity of outdoor recreation activities like tennis, skiing, jogging, snowmobiling, and bicycling has led to increased demands for recreation areas.

Another indication of the growth of recreation and parks can be seen by the number of colleges and universities that have initiated curricula in this subject area. Figure 1.5 represents recreation and parks as an academic discipline within institutions of higher learning. From 1930, when only one curriculum was in operation, the growth to over 300 in 1975 has been dramatic.

Today, the number of graduate and undergraduate students enrolled in recreation and park curricula in the United States and Canada number over 34,000. Less than 10 percent of that number were enrolled in 1960. Figure 1.6 indicates the rapid growth of students enrolled in such curricula during the years 1960 to 1975.

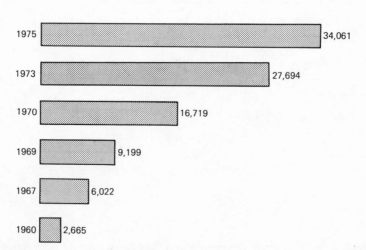

FIGURE 1.6   Number of Students Enrolled in Recreation and Park Curricula, 1960–1975

SOURCES: Sessoms, H. Douglas, "Education for Recreation and Parks Professions," *Parks and Recreation* **2**:12 (December 1967), p. 29.   Stein, Thomas A. and Roger A. Lancaster, "Professional Preparation," *Parks and Recreation* **11**:7 (July 1976), p. 60

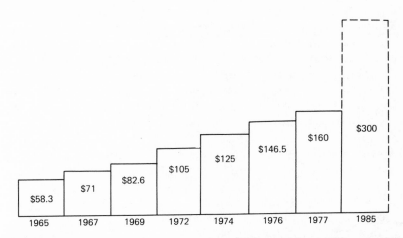

FIGURE 1.7   U.S. Expenditures on Leisure-Time Activities (Billions), 1965–
1985
SOURCE: U.S. News & World Report **82**:20 (May 23, 1977), p. 62.

As significant as the growth of municipal recreation and higher
education programs have been, so too are the substantial increases in
expenditures for recreation, parks, and related leisure items.

EXPENDITURES FOR LEISURE AND RECREATION

The cover story of the May 23, 1977, issue of *U.S. News & World
Report* states that leisure activities have become the nation's biggest
industry, with expenditures for leisure goods and services reaching
$160 billion. As indicated by Figure 1.7, leisure spending has risen
from $58.3 billion in 1965 to $160 billion in 1977. The economic staff of
U.S. News & World Report estimates an expected climb to $300 billion
by 1985.

Private Spending

A detailed account of consumer spending on recreation in the United
States during the late 1960s is provided by Richard Kraus:[10]

Books, maps, magazines, newspapers and sheet music	$ 5.6 billion
Nondurable toys and sport supplies	3.9
Wheel goods, durable toys, sports equipment, pleasure aircraft, and boats	3.4

Radio and television receivers, records, and musical instruments	7.4
Radio and television repair	1.2
Camping equipment and supplies	5.0
Swimming pools and accessories	1.0
Equipment and supplies for home "do-it-yourself" activities	12.0
Motion picture houses, gross receipts	1.9
Admission to legitimate theaters and opera, and entertainment of nonprofit institutions	0.6
Spectator sport activities	0.4
Gross receipts, of clubs and fraternal organizations, including dues and fees	0.9
Commercial participant amusements	1.6
Other purchases and fees	2.4
Parimutuel betting on horse racing	5.4
Travel for pleasure	37.0
Home entertainment	7.0
Alcoholic beverages, tobacco, and smoking supplies	23.7
Hunting and fishing	4.0
Lawn and garden supplies and equipment	2.0

$125.9 billion

Moreover, Thomas Watters chronicles recreation spending in the United States by pointing out that:
1. Total sales for the boating industry rose from $905 million in 1950 to an estimated $4.5 billion in 1975.
2. The sales of tents and sleeping bags nearly doubled between 1960 and 1970. Recreational camping vehicle sales increased by 400 percent from 1961 to 1970.
3. In 1962, less than 10,000 snowmobiles had been built in North America. By the end of 1971, there were over 1.3 million in operation.
4. At the conclusion of World War II, there were approximately 50,000 snow skiers in the United States. There are now almost 4.5 million skiers who will spend in excess of $2 billion on this activity.
5. Travel expenditures alone are anticipated to exceed $100 billion in 1978, almost 20 percent greater than all leisure spending in 1969.
6. In 1967, 3.5 million people played tennis, and spent over $22 million on equipment. The U.S. Lawn Tennis Association predicts a yearly growth calculation of 17 percent. Therefore, by

1980 these figures should increase to 53.2 million players who will spend almost $335 million on tennis equipment.

7. In 1971, $4 billion was spent on spectator activities, double the $2 billion spent on these activities in 1967.[11]

No matter which estimate of consumer spending on leisure one accepts, it is clear that all of the estimates are conservative since none of the total figures include such items as second home purchases, expenditures on capital construction of private and commercial recreation facilities, or government expenditures on cultural facilities.

Government Spending

It is estimated that in 1972, U.S. government spending on recreation was over $3 billion, while Canada spent over $900 million (see Table 1.1). These figures represent only the direct operating and capital expenditures of agencies with primary responsibility for recreation services. If other agencies who have a secondary or tertiary responsibility for recreation services such as forestry, fish and wildlife, armed forces and others are included, it is estimated that the gross recreation expenditures would rise to over $6 billion.

The rise of local expenditures for recreation (Figure 1.8) continues in spite of economic uncertainty and severe budgetary limitations. With this unparalled growth of recreation and park sponsorship, facilities, education, personnel, and expenditures, what guarantees does the public have that these efforts indeed have been effective?

TABLE 1.1 Government Expenditures on Recreation in 1972

JURISDICTION	UNITED STATES	CANADA	TOTAL
Federal	$ 563 million	$215 million	$ 778 million
State/Province	614 million	195 million	809 million
Local	1,991 billion	512 million	2,503 million
Total	$3,168 billion	$922 million	$4,090 billion

SOURCES: Bureau of Outdoor Recreation, U.S. Department of the Interior, *Outdoor Recreation: A Legacy for America* (Washington, D.C.: U.S. Government Printing Office, 1973), pp. 56, 68, 76. Statistics Canada, *Federal Province and Local Government Finance*, 3 vols., Ottawa, Information Canada, May, July, August 1974, pp. 16, 24–25, 30–31.

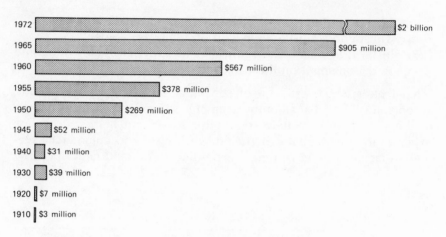

1972		$2 billion
1965		$905 million
1960		$567 million
1955		$378 million
1950		$269 million
1945		$52 million
1940		$31 million
1930		$39 million
1920		$7 million
1910		$3 million

FIGURE 1.8   U.S. Expenditures on Local Recreation, 1910–1972
SOURCES: National Recreation and Park Association. *Recreation and Park Yearbooks, 1956, 1961, 1966.* Bureau of Outdoor Recreation, U.S. Department of the Interior, *Outdoor Recreation: A Legacy for America* (Washington, D.C.: U.S. Government Printing Office, 1973), p. 76.

ACCOUNTABILITY FOR PUBLIC RECREATION PROGRAMS

As the level of expenditures for public recreation and park programs increases, so too do the demands of politicians and concerned citizens that there be increased productivity in the public sector, coupled with greater program accountability. Administrators can no longer justify increased budget requests based upon increased program attendance.

In a democratic society, ultimate accountability is to the citizens who may be directly or indirectly concerned with the accounting of public programs. No longer is simply the provision of municipal services enough to justify continued support, as has been the case in education, health care, and other services over a number of decades. People have begun to weigh the values of municipal services against the degree of financial support committed to them. Historically, weak or ineffective programs have had infusions of additional resources in the belief that the greater the expenditure, the greater the program outcomes. One does not necessarily follow the other, however, as was evidenced by Neighborhood Youth Corps, Model Cities, and a number of other social action programs.

Competition between public agencies for funds has increased greatly. At the same time, there are budgetary constraints in public spending, and there is mounting pressure on program administrators not only to generate new activities, but also to justify those that have been in operation for a number of years. More than any other single factor, this need to justify program activity and fiscal expenditures in the political arena has created the demand for an assessment of public program effectiveness. As a result, the demand for public accountability of recreation and park programs has increased more rapidly than the ability of administrators to respond. Sound program evaluation provides administrators with information that aids in decision making. It may help answer a specific question about the program, or it may provide solutions to problems in programming. Evaluation, then, becomes a keystone to the delivery of leisure services.

SUMMARY

The growth of organized leisure services in the twentieth century has been dramatic. In many cases, it parallels the growth of leisure time available to millions of citizens as a result of an increasingly technological society.

The 1960s and early 1970s heralded an unprecedented expansion of recreation and park services, especially in the public sector. In many cases, budgets were doubled every 10 years, bringing about an increase in programs, facilities, and staff to meet the continuing demand. However, a short time later with the end of a wartime economy, serious unemployment, and an inflationary economy, the well spring of public expenditures began to go dry. One of the first municipal agencies to feel the effect of shrinking budget allocations was the recreation and park department.

The scarcity of resources caused the shift in emphasis to program evaluation. With sufficient resources there would be no need to choose among alternatives. No objective would compete with any other. The primary process for allocating resources is the municipal budget. The budgetary process provides the mechanism whereby public officials see how highly their programs are valued in the form of appropriations. Evaluation provides decision makers with information to make intelligent choices among competing program alternatives.

In light of voter support for legislation to limit local property taxes, such as California's Proposition 13, the need for accountability and evaluation of recreation and park programs must become an essential management technique. Leisure service administrators who wish to continue program development, building facilities, property acquisition, and adding staff must do so judiciously. There is little logic in unbridled growth of recreation and park resources without first determining the extent to which current resources and programs are effectively achieving their stated objectives. This, then, becomes the explicit rationale or purpose in evaluation of leisure services.

REFERENCES

[1] These figures were derived from the following sources: a. United States—$160 billion—*U.S. News & World Report* **82**:20 (May 23, 1977): 62.
b. Canada—$14 billion—*The Determinants of Demand and the Prospects for Leisure,* Ottawa, Industry, Trade and Commerce, May 1976, p. 33.

[2] *U.S. News & World Report* **82**:20, p. 60.

[3] Allen V. Sapora, "Evaluation of Park and Recreation Operations: Who Should Do It?" *Parks and Recreation* **4**:12 (December 1969): 35 (see also pp. 35–36, 50–51).

[4] L. Hale Meserow, David T. Pompel, Jr., and Charles M. Reich, "Benefit-Cost Evaluation," *Parks and Recreation* **1**:2 (February 1975): 29 (see also pp. 30, 40).

[5] J. David K. DeShane, "From My Corner It's Obvious: Programs Need Evaluation," *Recreation Canada* **21**:1 (February 1973): 3.

[6] Christine McLean and Charles R. Spears, "Leisure Programs: Quandry or Quality," *Parks and Recreation* **10**:7 (July 1975): 21 (see also pp. 23, 42–45).

[7] Charles H. Pierce, "Program Evaluation—Future Perspectives," *Recreation Canada* **30**:2 (April 1972): 26 (see also pp. 24–30, 35).

[8] Alvin Toffler, *Future Shock* (New York: Bantam Books, 1970), p. 289.

[9] Foster Rhea Dulles, *America Learns to Play* (New York: Appleton-Century Co., 1940), p. 348.

[10] Richard G. Kraus, "The Economics of Recreation Today," *Parks and Recreation* **5**:6 (June 1970): 20.

[11] Thomas Walters, "The Leisure-Time Market and Its Impact on the Economy of Our County," *Recreation Management* **16**:10 (December 1972): 50–51 (see also pp. 48–51).

2

PURPOSES OF
EVALUATION

Recreation and parks evaluation is intended for use in administrative decision making. These decisions often concern improving the quality of service for citizens, as well as determining appropriate cost-benefit ratios of programs and resources. Why is an evaluation study undertaken? The answer becomes crucial since most major program decisions made based upon such an assessment depend on the answer to this question. Specification of why an evaluation is required not only helps determine the type and amount of information the study may produce, but also may suggest specific methods of measurement.

Program evaluation is an often discussed but infrequently used technique. This paradox may appear contradictory in light of attempts to make recreation delivery systems accountable to the public and to the various levels of government that provide funding. Moreover, in the past few years a number of legislative bodies have authorized funds to be used exclusively for evaluating recreation programs. Phrases such as "cost-benefit ratio" and "program budgeting" appear frequently in the literature, and evaluation units are being established in a wide variety of social action programs. Yet, despite these trends toward accountability, only a handful of recreation programs operating at any level have undergone evaluation in any but the most cursory manner. As often as the need for evaluation is verbalized, it is seldom accomplished.

Unlike other research, program evaluation is judgmental—that is, it asks how well a program is doing what it is doing, does it do what it intended to do, and whether it gives good value to its sponsor. Carol Weiss suggests that evaluation research should ". . . measure the effects of the program against the goals it sets out to accomplish as a means of contributing to subsequent decision making about the program and improving future programming."[1] The process then suggests a continuum (see Figure 2.1) because recreation decisions should be based upon the process of (1) determining goals, (2) specifying objectives, (3) operationalizing the program, and (4) measuring program effectiveness. This continuum should in turn lead to improved pro-

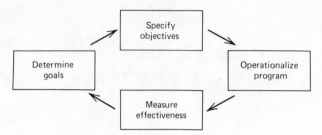

FIGURE 2.1 Evaluation Continuum

gramming based upon subsequent decision making. In the final analysis then, the purpose of evaluation in recreation is not to prove or disprove an activity, but rather to *improve* the conduct of that activity.

EVALUATION: OBJECTIVES AND SYSTEMATIC APPROACH

Objectives

One of the fundamental objectives of program evaluation is to determine whether a program or activity is doing what it is intended to do—that is, is it achieving its objectives? The initial step is to know what the specific objective is. Thus, program evaluation actually has two sets of objectives: the objectives of the evaluation process itself (research objectives) and the objectives of the program being evaluated (program objectives). These two sets of objectives are indivisible and often overlap, but they are not identical. In some cases, they are antithetical to each other.

It is understood that a fundamental objective of evaluation research is to determine whether the stated program objectives are being met. Some evaluators argue that a second and equally valid function of evaluation is to determine whether the stated objectives are indeed the actual objectives on which the program is operating, and, if so, whether the objectives are appropriate. Whether a program's objectives are or are not met (and the reasons for their success or failure), provides an excellent chance for the evaluator to look at the objectives themselves. Conceivably, some program objectives are not being met simply because the program participants do not identify them as their objectives. Often, administrators and program staff differ in the interpretation and basic priority of the stated objectives. Therefore, it is the responsibility of the evaluator to take the initiative in redefining or modifying the list of stated program objectives. This procedure then means that both the processes of planning and evaluation of programs must be circular in effect, constantly supporting each other as new information on program effectiveness is accumulated.

Systematic Approach

In the initial stages of program development a more precise definition of those aspects of evaluation must be made. The bottom line in the evaluation process is undoubtedly the determination of whether or not the objectives of the program are being realized. Traditionally, most recreation programs have been evaluated from a purely subjective approach such as asking: "Is the program successful?" The measure of success is determined by the instinctive feeling of the administrator that the program participants appear to be having a good time and are enjoying themselves. This "system" is purported to be dependent upon expert judgment, based on years of experience. However, the question of program objectives and empirical evidence of effectiveness play no role in this process. Normally, evaluation usually means a judgment of worth or value. When it is applied to both personnel and program it implies a comparative perspective as well. Evaluation also refers to a procedure or method by which precise and reliable knowledge is produced. When applied to a recreation program, the core elements of the following paragraph should evoke general agreement:

> The problem in evaluation [is] to provide objective, systematic, and comprehensive evidence on the degree to which the program achieves its intended objectives plus the degree to which it produces other unanticipated consequences . . . also relative to the agency. [2]

Within this statement, evaluation is one of a number of scientific research techniques, all of which share certain basic tenets such as the logic and design of research and the verifiability of findings. Research techniques differ mainly in their application to specific cases under investigation. For example, in a therapeutic setting, an experimental technique may be quite appropriate in measuring the effects of a recreation program on similarly disabled individuals. The same research technique might not be appropriate when measuring the effects of a recreation program in a municipal setting since it would be quite difficult to exercise control over intervening variables. The paragraph further emphasizes three elements: the nature of the data to be collected, the kinds of program objectives, and the manner in which the data are related to the objectives. This third element implies that evaluation consists of measuring the performance against predetermined program objectives. Stanley Bigman lists six uses of evaluation studies which expand upon the purposes of evaluation itself:

1. To discover whether and how well objectives are being fulfilled.
2. To determine the reasons for specific successes and failures.
3. To uncover the principles underlying a successful program.
4. To direct the course of experiments with techniques for increasing effectiveness.
5. To lay the basis for further research on the reasons for the relative success of alternative techniques.
6. To redefine the means to be used for attaining objectives, and even to redefine subgoals, in the list of research findings.[3]

What Bigman suggests then is that there is an inexorable relationship between evaluation and program planning, since each process relies on the other. We then move from a smaller continuum to a larger framework as exemplified in the Suchman process (Figure 2.2).[4] Wherever the point of entry, we must assume the previous step in the process has been taken. Usually, however, the initial step is value formation since goals are derived from values, whereas objectives are specified from general goals. The sequence of events suggested by Suchman can be illustrated by the following example. In a mental institution, if we accept the value that social groupings are better for people than isolation, we may then set as our goal that people shall participate in recreation programs as long as possible. We can measure our goal by determining how many people in the institution do not

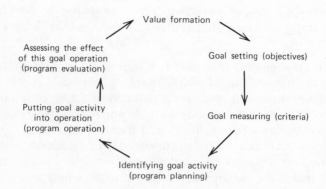

FIGURE 2.2 Evaluation Process

SOURCE: From *Evaluative Research: Principles and Practice in Public Service and Social Action Programs*, by Edward A. Suchman, Copyright 1967 Russell Sage Foundation, New York.

participate in the program. By identifying a measure of the goal, in-dicators will usually be determined that help attain the goal. A goal activity is planned such as the decision to assign recreation therapists to counsel patients at the intake-admission stage, on the assumption that early contact with patients will increase personal interaction. Next, we actuate the plan by assigning recreation therapists to patients at the initial stage. We now want to determine the effect of the goal-activity process, so we decide on an appropriate evaluation method-ology. If the investigation reveals that the program is working or not working well, it brings us back to the point of value formation.

TERMINOLOGY OF EVALUATION RESEARCH

Program evaluation may be designed to yield information about the total input (efforts), the total output (effectiveness) and the cost-ben-efit ratio (efficiency) in achieving the program's objectives. Program efforts are such variables as budget, staff, facilities, and equipment. Effectiveness on the other hand refers to the extent to which the program objectives have been achieved. Efficiency is the bridge be-tween efforts and effectiveness—the assessment of the input and out-put variables.

One of the barriers to understanding the evaluation process and the various methodologies of evaluation research is the imprecise and often variable terminology found in the literature. Because authors often use terms such as goals and objectives interchangeably, it is useful to focus on the definitions of terminology used throughout the evaluation process.

Research is that field of inquiry characterized by studies employing scientific methodologies in order to describe phenomena and/or to determine relationships between or among variables. It can be as simple as counting the number of cars or visitors using a state park, or as complex as determining the type and amount of behavioral change occuring to an emotionally disturbed individual as a result of a prescriptive therapeutic recreation activity.

Assessment is a process involving the utilization of both measure-ment and evaluation. For example, a community needs assessment for recreational swimming might include measuring the amount of time residents utilize pools and beaches in adjacent communities, the local temperature-humidity discomfort index, and, the number of drown-ings for the past 10-year period. After the data have been examined, a judgment is made relative to the costs and benefits of providing local resources for recreational swimming.

Measurement is the process of assignment of a number to some property of an entity. For example, measurement might include calculating the amount of community open space or determining a city-wide average of recreation participation in a given activity.

Evaluation concerns making judgments about the results of measurement in terms of specific objectives. For example, if after calculating the potential costs in terms of both time and persons necessary to remove litter from a public park after a rock concert, against the possible benefits to those in attendance, a recreation and park administrator makes a judgment about continuing or curtailing future concerts.

Monitoring is the continuous assessment of program objective achievement during the time the program is in operation. This process enables the administrator to follow the progress of a program and to make changes or modifications to it before it reaches completion.

Goals are something to reach out for, or ends to which a design trends. They may be an ideal and a value to be sought after, but are *not* an object to be attained. A universal or a statement of highly desirable conditions toward which a society should be directed can be a goal—for example, the elimination of boredom or the universal end to the work ethic.

Objectives are capable of both attainment and measurement. It is an aim or end of action, a point to be reached. An objective in recreation and parks might be the active participation of 50 percent of the city population in one or more municipal recreation activities during the course of a year.

Standards are prescribed criteria of acceptable, desirable, or optimum qualities or performances. They are usually established by consensus of expert opinion. A playground located no more than one-quarter mile from each home in a community or a minimum of $5.00 per capita spent for recreation and parks in every city are examples of standards.

ADMINISTRATIVE DECISION MAKING

The development and implementation of a recreation program requires the selection of specific courses of action from a variety of often competing alternatives. To make a choice among alternatives, the administrator must determine the relative values of each. For example, when faced with a operating budget cut, the recreation administrator may have to cancel or curtail one or more activities. To decide which specific activity will be affected, the administrator must be aware of both the activities themselves, and the impact of any impending action. The consequences of decision alternatives must be weighed and the activity that will minimize negative effects on the program should be selected. Therefore, it would seem natural for the administrator to define evaluation as the process of ascertaining the relative values of competing alternatives. Two concepts are paramount in the decision-making process: the utility of the desired products and the probability of achieving the desired result. The administrator seeks to maximize both entities—the utility and the probability. The utility of the product refers to the contribution it makes in moving toward the program goals and objectives if it is attained. Probability is largely a function of the amount and kind of resources expended on the related processes. It is assumed, however, that there exists a probability percentage for each desired outcome, above which additional resources will not be expended. The relationship between the probability of achieving the desired outcome or product and the amount of resources expended on it is likely to be unique and different for each particular program. For instance, a low-cost, small staff program such as ice skating on an open pond has a high desired outcome probability, especially if that activity has been successful in the past. However, a high-cost, large staff program such as a juried art exhibition may have a low desired outcome probability, especially if the activity is being conducted for the first time. The probability of achieving some outcomes will not be substantially changed by reallocating resources, while others are extremely sensitive to changes in the resource allocation level.

Case Study in Decision Making

The decision-making process usually includes four stages: (1) awareness that a decision must be made, (2) design of the decision situation, (3) choosing from various alternatives, and (4) taking action upon the chosen alternative. An illustration of this process would be the case of a sudden onset of vandalism within a city park. Although such cases may occur once in a long period of time, this example will be of a chronic repeated nature.

In the above example, our initial stage will be the decision execution, then we will proceed backward throughout the process. As will be seen, each step in the process will depend upon a prior step. The ultimate decision however, can be postponed, modified, or rejected at any point. The analysis is intended to demonstrate the need for evaluation information at every stage in the process.

The fourth or action step of the decision occurred when the recreation and park director ordered the park to be closed and the gates locked each evening after 6:00 P.M. and all day Sunday. While the critical part of this stage was the decision by the director, many other decision processes were required in order to carry out the order. Certain persons had to be assigned to open and close the park at designated times. The park supervisor had to meet with local citizens to explain what action was going to be taken and why. The media had to be contacted, police had to be advised to increase their patrols, and signs had to be changed to indicate the different hours of park operation. Finally, procedures had to be designed and implemented to assess the effect of the closing.

Before issuing the order to close the park, the director had to choose that alternative over others, such as hiring a guard or installing lighting throughout the area. This stage of the process is the choice stage, that is the act of exercising viable options.

Before making the choice to close the park, the director had to be aware of this alternative. This decision alternative may have been only one of a number of possible alternatives available. Before the chosen alternative was selected, it was necessary to identify or invent all other alternatives for consideration. A series of meetings and discussions may have been held by the director and staff to generate alternative plans of action. It should be understood that decision alternatives simply do not just emerge. They must be found or invented, and in order to assess them, they must be specified in operational terms during this part of the process called the decision design stage. Prior to the discovery or invention of the alternatives, the director had to be aware of the need for a decision. Awareness was brought about by reports from the park supervisor about the acts of vandalism. These reports led the director and the staff to the conclusion that the recreative experience of park users was being impaired. This is the decision awareness stage.

It is clear from this illustration that the decision-making process includes several stages, none of which is explicitly devoted to the provision of information. At each stage of the process information is necessary. The awareness that decisions need to be made is an essential and ongoing function of any evaluation program. To review possible courses of action, information is needed to determine costs, benefits, and probably success potential of the alternatives under consideration. While there are four stages in the decision-making process, each stage has several substages. The director did not want to merely select an alternative at random, so each possible course of action had to be considered carefully. This process in turn required information about each possible alternative. To obtain that information, the director and the staff had to determine criteria rules to choose the selected alternative. No doubt they also had to consider

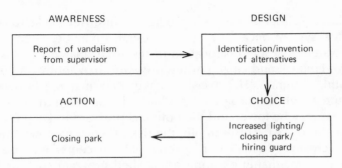

AWARENESS   DESIGN

| Report of vandalism from supervisor | ⟶ | Identification/invention of alternatives |

ACTION   CHOICE

| Closing park | ⟵ | Increased lighting/ closing park/ hiring guard |

FIGURE 2.3   A Decision-Making Model

the validity of the criteria rules once they agreed upon a particular alternative.

Figure 2.3 suggests a model for decision making based upon the illustration of vandalism. The four major stages: awareness, design, choice, and action relfect a process of increasing the rationality in decision making.

Probability

Evaluation research can also be viewed as a method of increasing the rationality of policy making. If empirical evidence on program outcome is obtained, sound decisions on budget allocations and program planning can be made. Programs that successfully meet their objectives may be expanded, while those that do not may be cut back or eliminated. As mentioned, two concepts in the decision-making process are vital: the utility of the desired outcomes and the probability of achieving the desired outcomes. The decision-making process seeks to maximize *utility* and *probability* by offering programs that have the highest success potential, at the least possible cost. The utility of a desired outcome is reflected in its contribution to the objectives of the program when attained. The probability of achieving the desired outcomes is primarily a function of the amount and kind of resources expended on the program. In most cases however, there is usually a probability ceiling for each desired outcome, above which cannot be exceeded by expending additional resources. The probability of achieving some outcomes may be substantially changed by reallocating resources, while others are insensitive to reallocation.

Decision makers often allocate resources for successfully established programs so that the probability of these programs attaining the desired outcomes is almost guaranteed. New or untried programs are riskier. Initially the risk factor is high because the real outcomes are unknown. In addition, new programs can upset the status quo of the entire system because ongoing programs may be so entrenched in the system that any reallocation of resources may present a threat to them. Political and citizen group pressures may lobby on behalf of an existing program. The decision maker then may not be willing to substitute a high-risk program for a low-risk one when the probability of success may be lower and the potential pressure to keep the status quo may be higher. For example, the risk of initiating a new program such as creative dramatics in a senior-citizen center may be much greater than maintaining a long established program such as bingo.

Utility

Along with the probability factor, the utility of desired outcomes is directly related to program goals. As goals change, so too do utility priorities for specific program objectives. Success probability and utility ratios may not be directly related; often they are in direct opposition of each other. New programs may have a low probability for success but a high utility priority. Established programs that have outlived their usefulness may have a high probability for success but a low utility ratio. The decision maker must make these difficult choices, especially when faced with limited available resources. One alternative is to play it safe by maximizing the probability for success by keeping the status quo, and to ignore the utility priority in relation to changing goals. A choice such as this ensures the stability and security of those within the system who might be affected by a shift in goals and reallocation of resources. However, creativity and innovation often are not accomplished by playing it safe. In the final analysis, utility priority should be a higher ranking factor for the decision maker than probability for success.

One of the barriers to efficient and effective recreation programs is politics played within and outside the system. It may be politically rewarding to maintain a program even when it has been demonstrated to have little effect on participants if the alternative is to do nothing for a certain group. Another part of the problem is the resistance of recreation organizations to unwanted information that might lead to unwanted change. Ineffective programs often are repeated over and over again. Organizations do not want information that may praise other programs but discredit theirs. However, the application of evaluation research methodology to recreation programs can lead to improved decision making, program planning, and more relevant and effective service delivery. Evaluation research will not eliminate politics from the decision-making process. If politics are viewed as compromise, negotiation, and accommodation, then this is the process of assigning values and priorities to facts.

Thus, the function of evaluation research is to provide specific information that helps eliminate uncertainty and clarifies the potential gains or losses that different decisions afford. It offers decision makers the opportunity to more effectively apply their values and priorities, with more accurate information on potential decision alternatives.

OTHER PURPOSES OF EVALUATION

There are a host of reasons to evaluate a recreation program, from the sincere and logical to the blatantly cosmetic. Successful administrators should question constantly their programs effectiveness. Are the programs doing what they are intended to do? Should they be expanded, cut back, or eliminated? Should more emphasis be placed on one activity at the expense of another?

Weiss suggests that administrators often have reasons, both overt and covert, for initiating a program evaluation. She proposes a number of situations when evaluation is done for the wrong reasons: postponement, avoiding responsibility, public relations, grant requirements, program justification, eliminating the administrator, and increased prestige.[5]

Postponement

When a difficult decision must be made, some administrators purposely procrastinate. In certain situations, such as issuing a permit to a controversial rock group for use of public recreation facilities, if the administrator waits long enough to decide, the problem solves itself. In our example, tickets must be printed and publicity must be released to the media. Most likely the rock group, pressed for time, woud seek other facilities. Another postponement method would be to pass the problem to a committee for study. This procedure may take several weeks or months. By then the decision situation may have died down or may no longer be necessary. In either case, the decision-making function is postponed until some future time period.

Avoiding Responsibility

Other situations demand that the administrator make a firm, but unpopular, decision. There may be only one course of action that the situation dictates, but the administrator does not want to be the one to make the decision. For example, if operating funds are insufficient to maintain the operation of a municipal swimming pool, there may be no other choice but to increase user fees. However, to avoid criticism of such a decision, the administrator may abrogate responsibility by initiating an evaluation study. If the evaluation study recommends an increase in user fees, the administrator has thereby avoided making the decision himself.

Public Relations

Good public relations are essential to public recreation programs. To convey a program's good image to the public, the administrator can commission an evaluation study in an attempt to inform elected officials and local citizens. If a positive evaluation report is forthcoming, the administrator will circulate the report widely: to the press, public officials, citizens' committees, granting agencies, legislative bodies, and others who can look upon the department more favorably. In contrast, negative evaluation reports are usually buried deep within the department's "archives." In some cases then an evaluation study can not only improve program effort, but also enhance the department's public image.

Grant Requirements

More funding sources are requiring evaluation studies of agencies receiving funds. Grantors want assurance that the monies they provide are being used effectively, especially in the case of untried projects. A widescale program outcome evaluation provides some evidence on the extent to which the program is achieving its objectives. Too often it is done under duress, which may lead to unfair pressures on the evaluators to furnish the granting agency with a positive report of activity when it may not be deserved. This is especially true with programs that have a high emotional appeal such as health, recreation, or welfare. A negative report, even where justified, may have serious repercussions in the community.

Program Justification

Whatever the source of operating funds for an organization, the administrator in order to increase the funding level often must justify the program to legislative bodies. This would include budget hearings at the local, state, provincial, and federal levels. A primary way to increase the yearly budget is to expand the program and accommodate more participants. The evaluation in this instance is that "more is somehow better," therefore accounting partially for ever increasing program attendance figures to justify increased budgets. In such situations the administrator must request a quantitative evaluation, stressing frequency and percentage of participation, rather than a qualitative one that might recommend cutting back or eliminating activities.

Eliminating the Administrator

The last covert purpose of evaluation is when a board or commission wants to fire its program executive, but due to community support, prestige, political contacts, or other reasons are unable to do so. An impartial outsider, however, may be just what is needed to accomplish this task—so an evaluation study is commissioned. The evaluator is told that "the program is only as good as the executive." Broad hints are given that no one in the community is satisfied with the program. Thus, the implication is not too difficult to follow, i.e., that the only way to improve the program is for the executive to resign. Too often the evaluator, hired by the board, recommends executive dismissal.

Increased Prestige

An evaluation often is done to increase an agency's prestige. This is especially true of programs that have, at best, only a marginal outcome when undergoing close scrutiny. An agency with poor programming, weak staff, or inadequate facilities, may commission a "selective" evaluation study. This type of study attempts to justify a weak program by only evaluating the strong or successful parts of the program. Or an agency may avoid any objective program appraisal in order to minimize or hide program failure. This may be accomplished by instructing the evaluator to interview a number of prescreened, predetermined board members, staff, and participants.

SPECIAL CONSIDERATIONS

The reasons for an evaluation study are of paramount importance since most critical planning decisions depend on that answer. Why an evaluation is required determines the amount and kind of information the study may produce, and it in turn affects the methodology of measurement.

Need for Evaluation

The first question is whether or not a program evaluation is necessary. The prerequisite in assessing this need and the form it should take is a clear understanding of the program's goals and objectives. Not all programs need extensive evaluation beyond what responsible administrators themselves are able to conduct on the basis of adequate data collection and reporting procedures built into the administrative system. However, a number of programs at some given point in time may benefit greatly from an impartial and objective evaluation. This perspective may be supported by special research skills, social science or other professional knowledge, and program administration experience beyond the level of specialist administrators.

For example, if a program administrator has had experience only in a single service program such as small, suburban community recreation agencies, the evaluation might be more comprehensive and meaningful if carried out by a more experienced evaluator, with a wider perspective to the provision of recreation service.

If the purpose of the program is specific and concrete, the program will be much easier to evaluate since the design may be tighter, more objective, and systematic. On the other hand, when program objectives are broad and more general, then evaluation becomes more difficult since the program variables cannot be controlled.

Program Effects

In the case where program objectives are specific and clear and results simple to measure, a study whose focus is based upon program effects may not be either what is needed or wanted. For example, in a specific aim program such as drop-in recreation center for youthful drug addicts, the main question may not be "what is the program achieving?" Instead, it might be more appropriate to investigate whether the initial problem still exists, whether it continues to exist in the same form or intensity, whether the population has changed, and to determine who is or is not benefiting from the program. Also, at what cost in relation to benefits is the program operating, and what additional or unintended effects is the program causing that may help or impede the realization of other desired ends. These factors are only in a broad sense program evaluation questions. They focus not on the measurement of results, but on broader program purposes and experience. The design of evaluation studies, therefore, may incorporate a variety of different approaches and skills, depending on what decision makers most need or want to know about the program.

Thus, some of the broader purposes that evaluation might accomplish include developing information about the change in extent and incidence of a problem, its cause, characteristics of participants, side effects of the program, and program efficiency. Additional evaluation investigation might include studies of public knowledge and attitudes toward the program and its impact, of administrative practices and the relationships between program personnel and participants, and of assumptions underlying the program objectives. Any or all of these factors may be critical to program performance and, hence, effectiveness in a given activity.

When to Not Evaluate

There are a number of occasions when serious questions should be raised about the efficacy of conducting an evaluation study. If the results of evaluation have no effect on the decision maker or the program itself, it should not warrant the expenditure of time and money. Tripoldi and others have suggested a number of circumstances when the evaluation decision should come under the closest scrutiny: [6]

1. When the objectives of the program are not clearly stated, it becomes unclear what is to be evaluated.
2. The degree of certainty of knowledge about the program's effectiveness must be considered because if the decision maker knows in advance that the program is working well, it is not necessary to evaluate.
3. If the program is being developed, possible changes in goals and objectives mitigate against conducting a study at that time.
4. If the disadvantages outweigh the advantages of doing an evaluation, it would be better not to proceed.

In addition to these occasions when evaluation studies must be considered carefully, they might also be counterproductive at other times. Evaluation studies require staff competent to conduct such research, as well as a commitment of funds to carry out the investigation efficiently and effectively. If either of these resources is not available, the chances of success are minimal. If a program is so flexible that it substantively changes from day to day, or if it has no specific focus or direction, it cannot be evaluated. Lastly, when the staff of an organization cannot come to an agreement on what the objectives of the program are, or what specific activities should be evaluated, the investigation should be postponed until such time when agreement is reached by those who will be affected by the study.

Mutual Understanding

Yet, given the circumstances above, what if the measurement of program results is still desired and needed? In such cases, it becomes essential that *before* commissioning an evaluation study decision makers and evaluators come to a clear and common understanding about what is expected to happen and when. If this step is not taken, the chances are that both parties will become increasingly frustrated with each other, and both will be dissatisfied with the evaluation results. It should be obvious that the risks of this happening increase as program objectives become more general and less specific, and as the time lag between the application of program activity and the accomplishment of the ultimate objective increases. Broad objectives and uncertain relationships between program means and ends inevitably lead to ambiguity between the conception of what the program intends to do and how what is done leads to the results sought.

SUMMARY

The most important question to be raised, again and again, is: Why is the evaluation study necessary? Since evaluation attempts to improve rather than to prove or disprove, the purpose of evaluation is to determine what is good and what is bad. The purpose of program evaluation is to find out the merits and shortcomings of the program. However, particular questions that concern participants, staff, and sponsors need more final judgments—these questions need information, interpretations, recommendations. A general overview of both merit and detriment may fail to address these questions. All parties involved in evaluation studies (1) need to examine the range of pertinent questions and to allocate what may be modest resources to those few questions that can be given primary attention, and (2) must consider not so much the definition or design of the study, but what they expect an evaluation study to accomplish.

It is important that a soundly conceived, written statement of the purposes or expectations of the evaluation study be determined. However, it is essential that all parties be satisfied completely that they know as much as they should about *why* the evaluation study is being undertaken.

REFERENCES

[1] Carol H. Weiss, *Evaluation Research: Methods of Assessing Program Effectiveness* (Englewood Cliffs, N.J.: Prentice-Hall, 1972), p. 4.
[2] Herbert H. Hyman, Charles R. Wright, and Terence K. Hopkins, *Applications of Methods of Evaluation: Four Studies of the Encampment for Citizenship* (Berkeley, Cal. University of California Press, 1962), pp. 5–6.
[3] Stanley K. Bigman, "Evaluating the Effectiveness of Religious Programs," *Review of Religious Research*, vol. 2 (Winter 1961): 99.
[4] Edward A. Suchman, *Evaluation Research: Principles and Practice in Public Service and Social Action Programs* (New York: Russell Sage Foundation, 1967), p. 34.
[5] Carol H. Weiss, *Methods of Assessing Program Effectiveness*, pp. 11–13.
[6] Tony Tripoldi, Phillip Fellin, and Irwin Epstein, *Social Program Evaluation: Guidelines for Health, Education and Welfare Administrators* (Itasca, Ill.: F. E. Peacock Publishers, 1971), pp. 114–15.

3

PROBLEMS IN
EVALUATION RESEARCH

A distinguishing characteristic of public recreation programs has been its focus within a community setting rather than in a laboratory setting. Research within an action-oriented setting creates problems of controlling variables, such as differing participants, staff changes, seasonal variations, and other program differences. The researcher cannot carefully control and manipulate all the variables in a community. Program participants are often diverse and unpredictable—from the preschooler to the senior citizen—thereby thwarting the researcher's attempts to construct a "pure" design for recreation program evaluation.

A general critique of evaluation research in recreation and parks today suggests that too few evaluation studies are being conducted, and those that have been made are generally of low quality.[1] The assumption is that the majority of recreation and park programs are not based upon, nor provide for, an evaluation of their effectiveness. In fact, most new programs fail to even include a plan for future evaluation.

Although an urgent need exists for better evaluation research in recreation and park programs, there are very few viable alternatives to the methodological problems faced by the researcher. In general, the wide range and variation of what is classified "evaluation," the absence of a clear-cut definition of either the objectives or methodology of evaluation research, and the variety of users of evaluation studies tend to make an already complex task more difficult.

It is absolutely essential to recognize that evaluation, by its very nature, must be concerned with possible change in an existing program. A precondition for evaluation occurs when (1) there is uncertainty about a particular program, and (2) a there is demonstrated need to reduce or eliminate that uncertainty. Evaluation is least likely to occur when: (1) there is disagreement about the desirability of evaluating the program, (2) there is a misunderstanding of the purpose of the evaluation, and (3) there is disagreement regarding the use and possible consequences of the evaluation. In addition to these problems, other considerations add to the difficulties of evaluation.

PROBLEMS IN EVALUATION STUDIES

Differences in Programs

One of the fundamental objectives of program evaluation is to determine whether a program or activity is doing what it is intended to do. However, one of the primary obstacles in the evaluation of recreation and park programs is individual differences among and between the goals and objectives of agencies and the programs themselves. There is no one way that agencies and institutions deliver leisure services, nor are the services (programs) themselves necessarily the same. Leisure programs are of many different types and cover a number of different disciplines. For example, leisure programs are sponsored by municipal government, public school systems, industry, and a number of voluntary agencies. Certain programs are related to delinquency prevention, while others are concerned with the maintenance or rehabilitation of mental health.

Programs also vary in purpose, objective attainment, structure, location, number of participants, and time span. These variations are extremely important in determining the most effective type of methodology. An evaluation that measures the effect of a senior-citizen outing would be inappropriate to measure the effects of a federal funding program for regional park development. The former program would be short-term, specific, and well defined, whereas the latter would be more complex, involve different purposes, more staff, and a substantially longer time span. Just as there are differences in programs, so too are there differences in the evaluation methodologies that must be selected and used to measure outcome effectiveness.

Purpose.   What the program is intended to do may be specific and well defined. For example, additional sites can be added to a campground to accommodate more participants. Other programs too may be specific and well defined such as teen drop-in centers, but staff differences may arise in supervision or administration. Although programs such as free-play activities, physical recreation, or leisure counseling are often extremely different, diffuse, and even difficult to describe, they must be described, even in general terms, for a program evaluation.

Objective Attainment.   Some programs attempt to effect change within individuals. For example, a crafts instruction program may improve manipulative abilities of physically impaired children, provide a potential source of income to skilled individuals, or simply provide relaxation for participants. Other programs ascribe to more complex goals that are difficult to define and measure, such as improving mental health, instilling esthetic values, or reducing juvenile delinquency. A goal such as "improving the harmony between humans and nature" carries with it a number of inexplicit subgoals that often are impossible to conceptualize and measure. In addition, short-term goals that seek to produce rapid change, such as physical recreation skill acquisition, are essentially easier for the evaluator to cope with than long-term goals, such as eliminating social distance between ethnic groups.

Structure. A recreation and park program like leisure counseling is so new and different that it provides a radical departure from usual programming patterns. More traditional programs, such as basketball leagues, can be found in most departments or institutions. Therefore, individual program characteristics will determine in large measure the type of evaluation to be conducted and the needs that evaluation may serve.

Location. The program being evaluated may be found in a single city hospital, a statewide park system, or it could be a national program such as scouting, ski patrol, or another primarily recreation program. Large-scale regional or national programs pose a more complex problem to the evaluator in terms of time, staff, and budget than do individual programs within one geographic area.

Number of Participants. A little league baseball recreation program may involve millions of children throughout the country, while another may service only a handful of individuals in one small community. The number of participants often dictates the methodology to be utilized in program evaluation since an interview technique might be appropriate only for a small number of participants. An alternative method would be feasible for larger numbers of participants.

Time Span. The recreation and park program time span can be a few minutes, a few hours, daily, weekly, monthly, or it may go on without interruption. One program may be a special event such as the U.S. bicentennial celebration; another might be an ongoing program like scouting, which no doubt will continue in the forseeable future.

Differences in Values

One of the major responsibilities of the decision maker is to make choices among competing alternatives. The major purpose of evaluation is to provide information that helps the decision maker choose a course of action. Evaluation then seeks to measure "what is" against "what should be."

Once the objectives of the recreation program are made clear, specific, and measurable, the question then becomes a matter of choosing which objective(s) to evaluate. Objectives are formulated on the basis of values, either explicit or implicit. Without values, there can be neither objectives nor programs. Values may be quite general such as "I believe in harmony among people" or "Society must provide for the needs of the aged," or they may be as specific as "those who have been in mental institutions have the right to equal employment opportunities," or "Former patients should have equal employment opportunities since they are individuals, and all individuals have human rights that should not be violated."

Differences in objectives often arise because of competition or differences in values. In teen-age social recreation programs, some individuals may believe that its value is its ability to teach social skills to youth, while others see its potential in reducing the amount of juvenile crime. Youthful participants may value the program for its opportunity to meet with their peers to discuss mutual problems. Each of these values may lead to different ideas of the appropriate objectives for teen-age social recreation programs. Discussions about these objectives will not be productive unless and until the differences in values are made known.

The next step in the evaluation process is to decide which objective(s) are to be measured. This decision should be based upon established criteria that will maximize the results of evaluation and minimize the fiscal and physical resources to be used.

Resource Constraints.   As with any program of research, there are certain limitations placed upon evaluation studies. When attempting to measure program effectiveness, the evaluator must determine how much time, money, and staff will be committed. Program administrators are often reticent about allocating resources to evaluation studies since many feel that these resources must be taken from day-to-day program operation. Competition then arises between what the administrator and the evaluator perceive as essential program elements. The administrator is responsible for operating the program, while the evaluator is responsible for measuring how well it is operating. The administrator must recognize that the evaluator is not working at cross purposes, but rather is attempting to furnish more specific information with which to make critical program decisions. The evaluator on the other hand must recognize that within any agency the funding, staff, and time available for the study are limited.

Objective Constraints. Certain recreation programs seek to achieve results rather quickly, while others cannot be achieved for a number of years. In a community near water, a number of drownings can prompt the local recreation agency to initiate a swimming instruction program. The goal may be to make every citizen in that community safe and cautious while in, out, or near the water. The objective may be to enable every child in grade six to successfully complete a Red Cross beginner swimming course. Results for sixth graders may appear quickly, but it would take years before a large portion of the community had the opportunity to participate in such a program. However, which is more important: the long-range goal of making every citizen safe or the short-range objective of starting with a single group? Decision makers usually want quick answers to questions and seldom will commit themselves to a study that measures a program's long-term effectiveness. It is important to determine what immediate effects a program has, but it must be recognized that these effects could change over time. Program evaluation to be most effective must measure outcomes on a long-term or continual basis in order to provide definitive information about how, when, where, and at what rate outcomes occur.

Another conflict that may occur in program evaluation are the differences between overt and covert objectives. Many administrators work on the basis of some covert objectives, whether consciously or subconsciously. Covert objectives often are compatible and without conflict in the overt goal structure of the program. However, there are times when these objectives do conflict between personal and institutional needs, or as a result of incompatible values held by various community groups. For instance, conflicting objectives may arise when the local recreation planning staff wants additional baseball fields, but the local residents favor a swimming pool. The recreation department may view more fields as enhancing their baseball program, while the residents simply may want a place to cool off during the summer. When such group conflict arises, an impartial, third-party evaluation of potential alternatives is often initiated. The pressure of the situation may compel such action.

Some recreation and park administrators have had favorable experineces with evaluation research, but usually the majority support is based on hope rather than experience. Few administrators have had either good or bad experiences with formal program evaluation studies. They become painfully aware of how little is known about their programs, how complex the problems are, and how elusive the solutions are. They are, as a group, highly conscientious about the effectiveness of their programs, and about doing what is best for the participants in those programs. Administrative desire to use rational management methods to improve programs is demonstrated by benevolent concern and long hours of preparation.

Granting Agencies

More and more pressure and initiative for conducting evaluation studies emanates from foundations or granting agencies. In the case of federal, provincial, or state agency funding, grant recipients assess program effectiveness as a requirement or condition of an initial grant or to continue funding.

Granting agencies are concerned that their money is well spent, especially in the case of new or untried programs. They recognize that creative or innovative recreation programs are essential, but they expect positive results. Recreation administrators on the other hand want to maintain preexisting programs. Their concerns center around staff, facilities, and equipment; they view evaluation as a necessary evil rather than an essential program component. Many administrators feel that evaluation regulations impede program operation, thereby placing it in a low-priority category within the department.

STANDARDS AND OTHER YARDSTICKS

Standards are the most widely used statistical methods in recreation and park programs today. However, standards should not be confused with norms. A *norm* is a series of statistical facts about a defined group of people, places, or events. Norms tell us what *is*; standards tell us what *should be*. Within the leisure-service field, standards have been established for the amount of recreation and open space that should be provided within a community, the ratio between staff to participants in aquatic programs, the adequacy of recreation areas and facilities, the education and experience qualifications of staff members, the location of playgrounds, and a number of other components that constitute programs within recreation and park agencies today.

There is a general agreement that the goal of recreation is excellence. How departments and participants should excel, and at what sacrifice, will always be debated. Whether goals and objectives are local, regional, or national, the measurement of excellence requires explicit rather than implicit standards.

Recreation and park programs have been subject to "standard-oriented" evaluation. Standards may be viewed as benchmarks of performance that have widespread reference value. Supporters of such standards as the National Recreation and Park Association's *Evaluation and Self-Study of Public Recreation and Park Agencies*[2] suggest that this type of checklist approach is relatively inexpensive, requires few research skills, and allows for comparison with other similar departments on a large-scale basis. However, even though recreation departments may use this same instrument, the interpretation of the listed data are often couched in inexplicit, personal terms. Data are usually presented in quantitative form, with little or no qualitative assessment indicated.

There is little knowledge anywhere today of the quality of a recreation program or of the behavioral change a participant undergoes as a result of the recreation program. Assessments usually are based upon predetermined criteria and standards of individual recreation leaders. An assessment used by the Milwaukee Public Schools, Department of Municipal Recreation and Adult Education, is presented in Figure 3.1. A leadership estimate is based upon 11 qualities of the recreation worker.

The majority of personnel or staff evaluation instruments compare a recreation leader with respect to other leaders, rather than examine the level of individual competence with respect to essential duties. Although most recreation leaders are competent to conduct activities, few have the ability to describe the participant's behavioral change as a result of that activity.

Checklists

Another evaluative instrument is the program checklist. These devices provide a given number of responses to one or more questions relating to the effectiveness of a program or activity. Typically, they are posed in a closed-end sequence, and a few provide one or two open-end questions that seek to elicit overall general responses. They usually take only a brief period of time to complete. A short response time increases the potential number of responses. However, the major disadvantages of this technique are the lack of comprehensiveness or detail in the potential responses and the multiplicity of interpretations that may result from the statements. Even when recreation checklists are interpreted correctly, evaluation is complicated by a multiplicity of standards. The sample checklist in Figure 3.2 was used during a recent recreation conference sponsored by the National Recreation and Park Association to gather participant information relating to the effectiveness of individual educational sessions.

Milwaukee Public Schools

Department of Municipal Recreation and Adult Education

Estimate of Worker

QUALITIES	SUPERIOR	VERY GOOD	GOOD (Average)	FAIR	POOR	COMPLETELY LACKING
1. General Influence—consider ability to foster normal values by setting a proper example and to imbue others with constructive and lasting attitudes.						
2. Personality—consider how favorably others are impressed.						
3. Cooperation—consider success in maintaining an effective working relationship with supervisor, fellow-workers, neighbors, other agencies, and the neighborhood.						
4. Program Organization—consider ability to intelligently plan a program with due regard for values and needs of the various individuals and groups, and to plan for effective use of individuals and groups in program conduct.						
5. Program Leadership—consider ability to direct, guide, and carry out the planned program by teaching and developing leadership within the group.						
6. Administration—consider ability to direct and manage according to the rules, regulations, and policies of the department.						

7. Initiative—consider ability to get better results by originating new ideas, trying new methods, and working effectively without detailed instruction.

8. Control (Discipline)—consider ability to control action of individuals and groups for the best interest of the individual and society, and consider judgment in using available aids.

9. Reliability—consider punctuality in submitting reports, fidelity in observing schedules, accuracy in statements and reports, and dependability in carrying out instructions and commitments.

10. Professional attitude—consider effort toward self-improvement, understanding and appreciation of the function of the department and the purpose of the program, interest and loyalty to the department, and discretion in discussing it and its policies.

11. Health—consider general physical health and emotional stability.

Rated By ....

FIGURE 3.1 Standards of Assessment

SOURCE: Division of Municipal Recreation and Community Education, Milwaukee Public Schools.

NATIONAL RECREATION AND PARK ASSOCIATION EVALUATION FORM, 1977 CONGRESS
FOR RECREATION AND PARKS

Just 60 seconds of your time will help us and help you. Please evaluate this Educational
Program completing the information requested below. Leave this form with the room host
or session moderator at the close of the session.

(1) Title of Session (Please Print) ....
....

(CIRCLE ONE NUMBER FOR EACH ITEM BELOW)

(2) Day   1   2   3   4   5
            SUN   MON   TUE   WED   THUR

(3) Time   1   2   3
              ALL DAY   MORNING   AFTERNOON

(4) My overall impression of this educational program was:
        Excellent   5   4   3   2   1   Poor

(5) The CONTENT of this program was:

Important   5   4   3   2   1   Unimportant

(6) The PRESENTATION of this program was:

Effective   5   4   3   2   1   Ineffective

(7) The PHYSICAL ARRANGEMENTS were:

Satisfactory   5   4   3   2   1   Unsatisfactory

(8) The amount of NEW INFORMATION I learned which will help me professionally is:

Significant   5   4   3   2   1   Insignificant

(9) NRPA Branch Affiliation (circle one)

1. AFB   2. APRS   3. NCSP   4. Student Branch

5. NTRS   6. SPRE   7. CBM   8. Nonmember

(10) Comments on this Educational Program: ....

....

(11) Comments on other aspects of the Congress: ....

....

FIGURE 3.2   Sample Evaluation Checklist

Since standards may vary from participant to participant, from recreation leader to recreation leader, and from department to department, the evaluator must be aware of which standards are held and by whom. Generalizations to a local recreation program from a universal standards approach is a poor research investment since differences in program objectives being compared is likely to be sufficiently great to negate any meaningful interpretation.

Patterns of Change

The concept of uniformity which standard approaches tend to perpetuate are simply not functional for individuals or agencies because leisure patterns and the delivery of leisure services are rapidly changing. Driving for pleasure was, until recently, the first choice of outdoor recreation activity for Americans. With the advent of an energy crisis, gasoline shortages occurred, recreation vehicle sales decreased, and the costs of fuel rose dramatically. The driving habits of the American people have been seriously affected. In addition, recreation departments like other municipal services have been affected by a shrinking dollar. Programs have been cut back and recreation administrators are being asked to provide more services with less money. Standards for recreation should then be viewed as ". . . only an educated, human opinion based upon long experience."[3] Such standards as one tennis court per 2000 people, a playground within a quarter-mile radius of every home, and a regional park within one-hour's driving time are only guesswork. In the final analysis then, standards and the support for such an approach are based upon history and past experience, rather than on any empirical evidence.

Professional Judgment

Other examples of evaluation approaches would include the professional or expert judgmental approach. Although these approaches are neither comprehensive nor objective, historically they have been a widely used strategy in recreation, typified by the use of "experts" to professionally judge a particular phenomenon. Examples of this approach are oral examinations at institutions of higher learning and state recreation societies for candidates seeking certification, panels of experts to review grant applications for government studies, and site visits by practitioners and educators to colleges and universities seeking accreditation of their curriculum.[4]

Often, a combination of the standards approach and expert judgment is used to arrive at checklists as criteria measures for program evaluation. Both standards and expert judgment, whether used separately or in combination, are not usually outcome measures, but rather guidelines of good practice as popularly accepted. The main emphasis of the expert or professional judgment approach to evaluation is the application of presumed expertise to yield judgments about quality or effectiveness. These measures, however, are not related to evaluation research since they related to program *input* rather than on outcome. One of the distinguishing characteristics of evaluation is its opportunity to test whether expert judgment and/or standards are in fact related to successful program outcomes.

TIME AND FINANCIAL CONSTRAINTS

The effective use of evaluation studies may be enhanced or, alternatively, hampered by a number of practical problems. A great many of these problems are related to the environment in which the study is conducted and the relationship among the evaluator, the agency, and its staff. Recreation programs are almost always conceived and initiated by policy makers or administrators without any involvement of evaluators. The planning process according to Caro should precede the actual program and should involve four elements:

1. Identification of problems.
2. Specification of objectives.
3. Analysis of the causes of problems and the shortcomings of existing programs.
4. An examination of possible action alternatives.[5]

The planning process should involve the evaluator whose work is concerned with and depends upon each step in the process. While it is recognized that evaluation should be built in to the program during the planning phase, an evaluation study itself should not be undertaken until the activity or program has had enough time to demonstrate its possible effectiveness. Of course, the program must be put into operation before it is evaluated. There may be occasions where the evaluation is limited to determining whether or not a program has succeeded in establishing itself, but this approach is extremely limited and cannot demonstrate program effectiveness.

While recreation programs should not be evaluated too soon, nor should they be evaluated too late. Evaluation should be conducted while there is still enough time to apply the results to the operation of the program. Recreation programs in some communities have been operational for so long that change is either no longer possible or can only be effected with maximum disruption and difficulty. New, innovative, or experimental programs such as detached, roving recreation leaders[6] have a much greater chance of success in evaluation since they are more subject to change than are such traditional, long established programs as basketball and other sports activities. The evaluation success possibility is higher in newly developed programs because it may be possible to "build in" evaluation research so that it can feedback information about that program. When evaluation research goes hand-in-hand with program operation, the result of the research can act as a quality control agent and can often redirect the focus or thrust of the program.

Time

A major difficulty facing recreation program evaluators is the time it takes to make a thorough and comprehensive evaluation. Often, however, recreation administrators want a quick or "one shot" evaluation of their program's effectiveness. This approach to program evaluation is naive and unrealistic since such short-sighted research, if undertaken, will almost never produce results that will demonstrate that a program is a total failure, nor that it is completely effective. The majority of recreation programs usually fall in between these two extremes, so it is absolutely essential that sufficient time be given the evaluation in order to improve negative program aspects and to increase its effectiveness. Evaluation research in recreation should be seen as a process whose focus of interest is the analysis of the total program process—that is, why it works or why it fails.

Funding

The second difficulty facing the evaluator is a lack of financial committment on the part of the recreation agency or administrator. Evaluation research costs money, and funds for research must come from operating budgets of recreation departments. In many communities, the recreation and park budget is underallocated, and available funds are expended cautiously by the administrator. Given the choice of spending even a small percentage on evaluation, the administrator usually prefers not to do so, because there would be less funds available for the program. An administrator's main concern is program operation; funds spent elsewhere will detract from the program output. However, this is a serious error since without some formal evaluation, the program may continue to operate, but how well it is operating remains an unanswered question. It is usually far better to have a fewer number of activities operating effectively, than more programs continuing on a hit-or-miss basis. The scarcity of financial resources makes evaluation research essential. If enough money were available to do everything, there would be no need to choose among alternatives. No single objective would be in competition with another. Therefore, evaluation is concerned with the allocation of limited resources among competing program activities.

POLITICAL CONSIDERATIONS

Unfortunately, even today, the majority of evaluation studies done in recreation and parks are filed away and forgotten. Rarely does an evaluation study have such an impact that it reaches the pages of the media and is reported on a large-scale basis. However, this may well not continue to be the case in the near future. More and more, legislation and administrative regulations may require the evaluation of programs such as recreation and parks where large sums of public monies are being expended. Evaluation in this instance may be due to governmental pressure for accountability and increased productivity.

The results of evaluation studies have always had political overtones since they yield conclusions about the worth or effectiveness of programs, which in turn affect the allocation of resources. The purpose of evaluation research is to measure program effectiveness, and the outcome of this study is one or more of the following recommendations:

1. To maintain the program in its present status.
2. To expand the program to a broader base.
3. To modify the program to help achieve its objectives.
4. To phase-out or abolish the program.

The first two alternatives concern programs that have been assessed as successful, while the last two relate to unsuccessful programs or activities. However, any of the above recommendations may well come under political scrutiny.

If an evaluation study is judged to have political significance, the results are often challenged by the individuals or groups who hold different views than that which the study indicates. One of the first methods of those who do not support the data is to find fault with the particular study methodology. Opponents can usually find experts to uncover faults in the hypotheses, purposes, sampling, design, statistical treatment, measurement, or interpretation of the data. In most cases these experts' criticisms are aimed more at the ideology of the study than its methodology. Evaluators must recognize that once such a study enters the political arena, they must be prepared for microscopic scrutiny of not only the recommendations, but also of the study methodology and procedures.

Consequently, friction may develop between the evaluator and the program staff, because staff members are concerned with operating the program and may resent any intrusion on the part of the evaluators who measure program effectiveness. Program staff who feel that an activity is doing well consider an evaluation unnecessary and a waste of time and money. If, however, the program has some difficulty (as most have at some time) and may show negative or no results, they may feel that the program and indeed their own job is in jeopardy. These feelings can lead to hostility and ultimately work against what is needed: improving the program's effectiveness.

Resistance to Evaluation

Finally, it must be understood that resistance to evaluation research is likely to increase if there is conflict between the goals and objectives of the program and those of the agency or organization seeking the evaluation. Organizations by their very nature tend to perpetuate themselves since their goals tend to be that of power, growth, stability, and survival. If these goals conflict with those of a specific program, a number of difficult problems will develop. For instance, one of the principal objectives of therapeutic recreation programs is to make each person ultimately responsible for meeting his or her own leisure needs. If this objective is accomplished, there would be no further need for a recreation organization. The evaluator must recognize that if the study results tend to weaken the power of organization, such results will probably be resisted. Even if the study results demonstrate that the organization has done such a good job in eliminating a problem that they may be in danger of putting themselves out of business, internal pressures will be exerted that will tend to seek a new problem area in order to justify continuation of the organization. There is a tendency for organizations to equate power with purpose, or even to place power above purpose, so that survival as an organization becomes an end in and of itself.[7] Watergate and the Office of the President are graphic examples of how the instinct for self-preservation is almost as strong among organizations as it is in individuals.

SUMMARY

There are a number of problems within the leisure-service field that make valid and reliable evaluation studies difficult to accomplish. Differences in programs, objectives, structure, location, participants, time, values, and individual constraints make it extremely difficult to make comparisons between agencies and their programs. In addition, the field of recreation and parks is dynamic rather than static, and that very dynamism reflects constantly changing patterns of service, thereby making it difficult to control or measure critical program variables.

The use of standards in leisure services with regard to facilities, staff, programs, equipment, and budget are common since they allow individual communities to see how they compare with others. However, the use of standards approaches tends to promote uniformity, and eventually mediocrity. Standards have only single criteria—if a community has reached the standard or not. There is no room for individual differences within communities, and rather than standards being considered as *minimums*, they instead become the desired level of achievement.

Very little time or funds are allocated to program evaluation by recreation and park administrators since many of them feel that these resources must be siphoned from the ongoing program. However, even with a scarcity of operating funds, program evaluation is essential in order to determine which activities are operating effectively. No matter what the problems are—physical, fiscal, or political—evaluation of recreation and park programs can provide the decision maker with essential information on the cost, distribution, and effectiveness of the program.

REFERENCES

[1] David K. De Shane, "From My Corner It's Obvious: Programs Need Evaluation," *Recreation Canada* **21**:1 (February, 1973):3.
[2] Betty van der Smissen, *Evaluation and Self-Study of Public Recreation and Park Agencies* (Washington, D.C.: National Recreation and Park Association, 1972), 69 pp.
[3] National Recreation and Park Association, *Outdoor Recreation Space Standards* (Washington, D.C.: The Association, 1965), pp. 17–18.
[4] The National Recreation and Park Association, in cooperation with the American Association for Leisure and Recreation, has recently

established a Council on Accreditation to accredit and publish a list of institutions of higher education so accredited. The Council sees accreditation not only as a means of ensuring educational standards, but also as a means of stimulating institutional self-improvement in colleges and universities that offer professional preparation programs in recreation, leisure services, and resources.

[5] Francis G. Caro, ed., *Readings in Evaluation Research* (New York: Russell Sage Foundation, 1971), p. 3.

[6] The roving recreation leader program refers to a leadership personnel system that deploys recreation leaders not to specific locations, but rather to various areas within a community where their services are needed most. They have been also referred to as "detached workers" since they move about under direction and supervision of the recreation department.

[7] Bernard Berelson and Gary Steiner, *Human Behavior: An Inventory of Scientific Findings* (New York: Harcourt, Brace, and World, 1965), pp. 366–67.

PART TWO

THE PROCESS OF
EVALUATION IN
RECREATION AND PARKS

4

FUNCTIONS OF
EVALUATION RESEARCH

Evaluation is an essential part of the leisure-service delivery system. As such, it becomes one of the most important components of administration. Traditionalists view administration as a process that includes the elements of planning, organizing, staffing, directing, and controlling an activity or a system of activities. Since the main concern of administration is the organization and management of resources and activities in order to achieve desired outcomes, and since evaluation research is the study of relationships between planned activity and desired outcomes, it is obvious that evaluation research is critical to the administrative process. Evaluation then is programmatic research since its main concern is to assist administrators and program personnel to plan and modify their activities in order to increase the potential of achieving program objectives.

EVALUATION USES AND APPROACHES

Evaluation studies have a number of specific uses. Knutson suggests ten examples for organizational evaluation:

1. To demonstrate to others that the program is worthwhile.
2. To determine whether or not a program is moving in the right direction.
3. To determine whether the needs for which the program is designed are being satisfied.
4. To justify past or projected expenditures.
5. To determine the costs of a program in terms of money or human effort.
6. To obtain evidence that may be helpful in demonstrating to others what is already believed to be true regarding the effectiveness of the program.
7. To support program expansion.

8. To compare different types of programs in terms of their relative effectiveness.
9. To compare different program methods or approaches in terms of effect.
10. To satisfy someone who had demanded evidence of effect.[1]

Posed as questions, these ten examples form a substantive basis or rationale for program evaluation. Faced with the demand for increased productivity and holding the line on public spending, evaluation of recreation and park programs then must furnish decision makers with information and alternatives to such questions as: Should a poorly attended program be continued or dropped? Should the approach to it be modified in some way? Should more or fewer resources be devoted to it? Should it be moved to a different setting? At what point should these decisions be made?

Scriven proposes two useful approaches to evaluation that afford greater flexibility, both for administrators and program personnel who seek to improve program effectiveness: formative and summative evaluation studies.[2]

Process Evaluation

Formative or process evaluation produces information during the course of program development or operation which is fed back to decision makers and which provides the opportunity to improve the program long before it terminates. Formative evaluation supplies data that may contribute to a series of decisions on specific aspects of a program, rather than on the overall decision. The process approach, therefore, indicates a willingness and a necessity to review much more in the way of evidence and alternatives than a simple comparison between the program objectives and its outcomes.

Outcome Evaluation

Summative or outcome evaluation, on the other hand, is done after the program has been completed and provides information about the overall effectiveness of the total program, measured against its stated objectives. Summative evaluation is particularly useful in providing a basis for decision making about program alternatives since the process is designed to measure which programs work and which do not.

Unfortunately, even with such a distinction between formative and summative evaluation, the majority of recreation and park programs do not utilize these approaches. Evaluation should be conducted both in the process of program development and operation, and therefore should serve simultaneously in a formative and summative way. Indeed, it is desirable to do so since if considerable resources are used in research, as much information as possible should be gained from the data gathered. It would be wasteful to investigate what some programs should achieve without looking also at how closely they are achieving their desired objectives. In addition, research should not only indicate whether or not objectives are being achieved, but also should furnish information on to the reasons why these objectives are or are not being achieved. In addition, evaluation research should suggest the relative appropriateness of various objectives in the context of the program's success or failure in meeting them.

THE QUESTIONS TO BE ANSWERED

The most clearly identifiable facet of evaluation research is the presence of some objective that when measured in terms of attainment is the principal focus of the research problem. Evaluation studies cannot operate in a vacuum. The question must always be asked, evaluation of what? Each activity or program in recreation has some value for some purpose, so it makes little sense to ask whether a program has any value, without specifying value for what. Values are translated into objectives. If these objectives are clear, specific, and measurable, then evaluation research can be accomplished.

The usual evaluation question is: To what extent is the program achieving its objectives? An evaluation study can be seen as the study of change. The program being evaluated is the causal, or independent, variable, while the objective is the effect, or dependent, variable. Placed in this context, the researcher may formulate an evaluation study in terms of hypotheses that state that activities A, B, and C will produce results R, S, and T. This hypothesis requires both a statement of end result, or program objectives, and the specification of what it is about the program that might be expected to produce these results. Other hypotheses might be: Is program A functioning better than program B in attaining their common objectives? What part of the program, F, G, or H, is having more success? No matter which hypotheses are utilized, the basic premise is the same—there are objectives, there is a program intended to achieve these objectives, and there is a measurement conducted as to the extent the objectives are achieved.

Problems of Definition

The initial issue confronting the evaluator is to determine a satisfactory definition of what exactly is to be investigated. Recreation administrators and program personnel often pose problems in vague and generalized terms that do not usually lend themselves to scientific study. Therefore, often the first responsibility of the evaluator is to analyze the problem and identify those aspects to be investigated.

Evaluators often differ on whether a fully developed hypothesis is necessary to test. When it is premature to construct a comprehensive hypothesis, an exploratory study should be undertaken to clearly define areas to which high priority must be assigned in a more rigorous investigation. As an example, the evaluator must look at the kind of questions that will be involved in evaluating the effectiveness of an inservice management training program for selected area supervisors in a municipal recreation department. The first, and perhaps the only, question posed to the evaluator may be: "Is the program effective?"

In this context, part of the evaluator's analysis is to examine the precise meaning of the word "effective." It may answer any one or a number of the following questions:

1. To what extent did the inservice training program modify or change the behavior and performance of the participants in doing their job?
2. To what extent did the program enable the participants to communicate more effectively with the recreation department?
3. To what extent did the course ensure that participants will remain in their job longer than those who did not participate in the program?
4. To what extent did the program result in more positive effects of the activity on the population served?

These examples are but a few of the varying criteria by which effectiveness can be judged. In addition, there are a number of other questions which the evaluator may wish to investigate including:

1. Are the participants involved in the inservice course different from other supervisors who have not had this training?
2. Is any difference in the participants really due to the effect of the training program, or is it merely due to the fact that they have been singled out for special attention and therefore given recognition?
3. Does the program have negative as well as positive effects, and, if so, what are these negative effects?

Evaluation studies must be related strongly and positively to the objectives and policies of the program undergoing evaluation. In the inservice training course example, evaluation should relate to the program for which these supervisors are being trained and the tasks which they are being prepared to perform.

Complexity of Evaluation

It would appear on the surface that all the researcher has to do in order to conduct an evaluation would be to determine the program's objectives, translate these objectives into measurable indicators of objective achievement, collect data on the indicators for the program participants, and compare the data on the participants with that of the objective criteria. Although this procedure appears simple enough, recreation and park programs are usually not as accommodating and neat as the evaluator would like. Often, outside circumstances intervene to make the whole process more complex. First, program objectives in recreation and parks may simply not exist, or they may be vague and abmiguous. Often, there are goals but not objectives, and these goals are so universal and full of platitudes they become meaningless. As an example, recreation administrators often suggest that their program goals are to enhance the quality of urban life, create a balance between humans and the environment, or improve community citizenship. Second, programs not only move toward stated objectives, but they often accomplish other things in addition to or instead of the objectives. A senior-citizen program objective may be to provide needed physical activity for participants. However, unplanned outcomes such as companionship, friendship, even love and marriage may result from the physical and social contact the program provides. The evaluator has the obligation of studying these unanticipated consequences since they may bear heavily on program outcome. Recreation programs are a blend of activities, facilities, equipment, staff, and participants, and while some elements are essential for the effect they achieve, others may be unnecessary or irrelevant. Program administrators have to know which are the basic and essential elements of the activity, so that if they are successful, they can repeat them, or, if unsuccessful, they can delete or avoid them. Often ignored, but nevertheless of major importance, is the question of *why* a program succeeds or fails. The answer to this question is sometimes more important than the answer to how well the program works. If evaluation is viewed as a process to improve rather than prove or disprove, an answer to the question of why a program failed may justify trying a new approach or reallocating resources for program improvement.

LEVELS OF INFORMATION UTILIZATION

There are a number of different operating levels within park and recreation organizations. Traditionally, when viewed from the bottom up, there is the recreation leader, then the specialist, the supervisor, then the administrator. The system can be enlarged if we include boards, commissions, and elected public officials. Each individual or group within this hierarchy has a function and certain implicit or explicit responsibilities. When conducting an evaluation study, the evaluator must fit in somewhere within the existing system—he or she is responsible to a person at some level of authority within the organization. If the evaluation study seeks to determine whether or not to enlarge, delete or modify the program, or to determine its overall worth, then the evaluator should report and be responsible to the policy-making level within the department. If the evaluation study seeks to determine which methods of operation, which organizational structure, which staffing patterns, or which promotional techniques to use, then the evaluator is concerned not with the overall program, but with specific features of an activity, and should report and be responsible to program personnel.

Problems can occur when the evaluator is incorrectly placed within the department. If the evaluation study is commissioned by the principal administrator or recreation commission, they are generally concerned with policy rather than operational questions. On the other hand, program personnel are primarily concerned with how effective activities are, so to them, operation is the essential element. What questions are to be answered, policy or program related ones, determines where the evaluator will be placed within that structure. Evaluators are frequently confronted with demands for information from a number of different individuals and groups. Parents want to know how well their children are doing in specific recreation activities. Program participants want to know how well they have performed in activities. Recreation leaders seek feedback from program participants. Recreation supervisors are interested in how well their programs are doing in relation to other, similar programs. Recreation directors want such data as the number of participants in each activity. Recreation boards, commissions, or elected public officials are interested in community attitudes toward recreation and the cost/effectiveness ratios of the department's programs. Clearly, to respond to each of these information requirements would be a monumental task.

If the evaluation is conducted for program staff, considerable pressure may be placed both on the evaluator and on the program staff to not report negatively on any aspect of the overall program. If this type of report is made, it may well be stalled or completely eliminated by those in policy-making positions. On the other hand, if the evaluation is conducted for policy makers, program personnel may be reluctant to participate since they may feel that the evaluator is checking on how well they are doing their job. In such a case, program personnel may withhold information from the evaluator, or make themselves unavailable, especially if program staff are convinced that their programs are being measured against others within the department. They may not be willing to offer information that may be construed as poor performance on their part, or increase competition among other programs which are vying for the same resources.

Multiple Use

The problem of evaluation location becomes most difficult when the study is designed or commissioned to serve multiple levels within the recreation department. In most cases, it is impossible to serve more than one level within the organization. The evaluator and the recreation department would be well served if the study were located at the policy level when potential conflict may result. Responsibility to the higher level enables the evaluator to maintain a greater degree of autonomy. However, the evaluator must enlist the cooperation of program staff to determine the critical issues in the daily program operation and incorporate these issues into the evaluation study. The evaluator must be viewed as a colleague, rather than an inspector checking up on leadership and supervisory staff. One method of accomplishing this task would be to involve from the onset of the study all personnel levels within the organization. Although the evaluator plans and coordinates the study, staff at all levels should be responsible for direct supervision of the study, depending on the study's scope and purpose.

Levels of Objectives

Program objectives usually are arranged in descending order—that is, the objectives make up an ordered series, each of which is dependent for its existence upon an objective at the next higher level. Each objective in turn is implemented by means of lower-level objectives. The policy-making staff within the organization assumes responsibility for the higher-ranking program objectives, and each succeeding lower-ranked staff is responsible for one of the intermediate objectives on a descending scale.

Consider a large metropolitan recreation and park department as an illustration. The ideal or ultimate objective of the department is to provide for the leisure needs of all citizens within the metropolitan area. A high intermediate objective for the recreation and park commissioner might be to provide a complete adult recreation program by coordinating commercial and private recreation services, offering a balanced departmental program of activities, and by providing leisure counseling. The recreation superintendent may adopt the initiation of a performing arts program within the community as the immediate objective. To implement this program, the recreation center director might involve all senior citizens who attend the center. The recreation specialist, in turn, has to determine which of the performing arts activities will have the greatest demand and interest. Finally, the recreation leader may be responsible for the objective of exposing all senior citizens to a music appreciation program. Each of these objectives can be evaluated, and studies may even be conducted at levels involving individual participants.

Recreation program evaluation works back up this scale of objectives. The degree to which an objective has been achieved, in turn, becomes a step toward determining the next higher objective. If each recreation leader in the above example does an effective job, this success contributes toward the determination of the appropriate activity by the recreation specialist. If the specialist does a good job, there is further progress toward the center director's objective of involving all senior citizens. This progression continues until the final evaluation of the entire program is sought by the recreation and park commissioner in order to determine how complete the adult recreation program really is. Seen in this light, all recreation programs can be divided into a series of events in which any individual action is the result of the one preceding it, and a necessary condition for the one following it. Evaluation research can then validate the relationships between each corresponding set of objectives that make up the recreation program.

Since evaluation works back up the scale of objectives, a cumulative series of events progresses from the lowest or most immediate objective toward the highest or ultimate objective. Figure 4.1 presents an example of sequential evaluation levels that measure leisure research literacy, using the *Journal of Leisure Research*.[3] This model has been adapted from Greenberg and Mattison's step chart of different levels of evaluation for health education literature.[4]

Intermediate objectives are based upon the premise that leisure research literacy will be affected if a prior series of events occur. The ultimate objective of increased literacy is based on three premises: (1) that the journal is available to a large proportion of individuals in the recreation and park profession, (2) that it will be read, and, (3) that it will have some effect in motivating individuals to read frequently

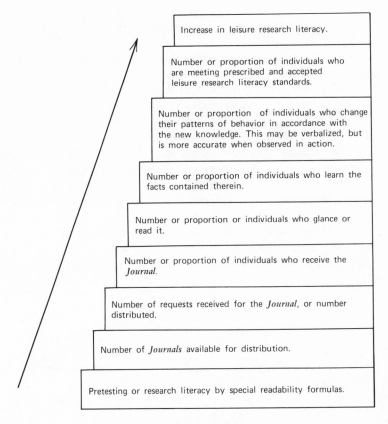

FIGURE 4.1   Evaluation Levels of Leisure Research Literacy with the *Journal of Leisure Research*

SOURCE: From *Evaluation Research: Principles and Practices in Public Service and Social Action Programs*, by Edward A. Suchman, Copyright© 1967 Russell Sage Foundation, New York.

and improve reading skills. There can be no doubt that secondary and intermediate objectives must be accomplished before attainment of the ultimate objective. If this was not the case, activity would take the place of effect, and the objectives that lead to the adoption of policies and procedures for implementation would be meaningless since the means would become ends in and of themselves. Even the most remote and secondary objectives must somehow be connected to the chain of events that moves toward ultimate objective attainment.

Aware of the inherent difficulties in conducting and utilizing evaluation studies at different information levels, we now consider the organizational arrangements for evaluation research.

IN-HOUSE VERSUS OUTSIDE EVALUATION

A basic administrative issue concerns the comparative advantages and disadvantages of employing evaluators from within the organization itself, or choosing outside evaluators who have had little or no exposure to the recreation and park department. Individuals or organizations commissioning evaluation studies are subject to criticism no matter which alternative they choose. In a political setting such as municipal recreation there is usually less skepticism and more confidence placed on evaluation personnel who are not part of the organization to be studied. Evaluation has been placed in the hands of individuals or organizations external to the program such as university departments, individual researchers, consultants, or other technical personnel. There are some situations where this is a viable strategy but many examples demonstrate that there are inherent difficulties with such an approach. The advantages and disadvantages of external evaluation can be seen as follows:

Advantages
1. External evaluators can introduce a higher level of objectivity and ability to view things that program personnel may take for granted.
2. Specialists have resources and knowledge that may not be available internally.
3. They have less direct involvement in the evaluation outcome and feel less pressure to make compromises in the research design or interpretation of results.
4. They may be better able to question basic organizational premises.
5. They may be better able to mediate internal organizational conflicts.
6. They may be able to make evaluative comparisons of similar programs based upon past experience.

Disadvantages
1. External evaluators may represent a threat to program personnel and thereby face staff resistance.
2. They are less likely to understand or grasp all the factors of the program and be less sensitive to the possible disruptions of the program as a result of the evaluation study.
3. They may slant their study interpretations to accommodate their client's interests so as to maintain good relations.

On the other hand, an organization may attempt to structure itself to provide for internal evaluation without outside assistance. In-house evaluation also has advantages and disadvantages:

Advantages
1. Internal evaluators may be more readily acceptable to the program staff, especially if the staff view the study as a self-appraisal for their own good.
2. They may be better informed about the program and know which aspects require evaluation.
3. They are in a better position to conduct continuing program evaluation.

Disadvantages
1. Internal evaluators face more pressure for positive results, thereby making it difficult for them to retain their objectivity.
2. They often focus their study on positive or successful aspects of the program at the expense of weak or unsuccessful ones.
3. They may not possess the required research skills and knowledge to conduct a thorough and comprehensive study.
4. They may not question long-standing organizational policies and procedures because they may interpret them as being valid.

The answer to who should do the evaluation depends largely on a number of specific criteria. On the other hand Nienaber and Wildavsky suggest that:

Evaluation and organization may be contradictory terms. Organizational structure implies stability while the process of evaluation suggests change. Organization generates commitment while evaluation includes skepticism. Evaluation speaks to the relationship between action and objectives while organization relates its activities to programs and clientele. No one can say for certain that self-evaluating organizations can exist, let alone become the prevailing form of administration.[5]

This description of internal evaluation tends to fall victim to the inevitable institutionalization of programs that occurs within organizations. Even if an organization establishes a high-level structure in order to provide evaluation information to its policy makers, the evaluation structure invariably becomes part of and is identified with the organization's overall programs and objectives.

Consequently, the best form of evaluation appears to be one combining both internal and external evaluators. Internal recreation personnel should formulate and define the program objectives and the activities to be evaluated. This activity should be done in consultation with the outside evaluator who should be encouraged to raise questions during the process. The outside evaluator then designs the evaluation study, in consultation with the recreation staff, and both groups attempt at the design stage to minimize any possible disruption to the program operation. The required data are collected jointly. The outside evaluator assumes the principle role in analyzing the data and presenting the evaluation results. Collectively, the findings of the study are translated into recommendations for program modification. The recreation staff then implements the recommendations.

In the final analysis then, whoever conducts the evaluation study—be it internal, external, or a combination—must possess the qualities of independence, objectivity, program understanding, research ability, and must have the confidence of the sponsoring organization that the study will be efficient, effective, and meaningful.

EVALUATION AND NONEVALUATION RESEARCH

Recreation and parks research has followed generally one of at least three different types of scientific inquiry: empirical studies, historical studies, or philosophical studies.

In empirical studies observations or experiments are used to describe existing conditions and prove or disprove claims, statements, or hypotheses about relationships between variables. A empirical study might measure attitudes of residents toward community recreation programs, determine carrying capacities of outdoor recreation resources, or measure the effects of a leisure counseling program. It is fair to assume that the overwhelming majority of research in recreation and parks are empirical studies.

Historical investigation generally studies the development of organizations, people, movements, or events. Examples of such inquiry in recreation and parks would include a history of the National Recreation and Park Association, the development of the playground movement, or the biography of the famous landscape architect, Frederick Law Olmstead.

Philosophical study is allied closely to rational analysis and is loosely based on formal logic and semantics. Studies to determine the morals and ethics of juvenile gangs, spectators at sporting events, and corrupt public officials are examples of this type of inquiry.

Evaluation and research are inquiry activities since systematic inquiry techniques are used, although for different purposes. While research attempts to produce new knowledge, evaluation attempts to judge worth, utility, or effectiveness. Collectively evaluation research utilizes the scientific method to collect data concerning the degree to which a specified activity produces some desired effect.

Basic and Applied Research

There is a further distinction to be made when research is considered as an inquiry process: whether the research is *basic* or *applied*. Some researchers feel the distinction is more a matter of purpose than method since the great majority of research has both basic and applied elements. However, the distinction helps in subsequent consideration of evaluation research. The National Science Foundation has proposed the following definitions:

> *Basic research is directed toward the increase of knowledge; it is research where the primary aim of the investigator is a fuller understanding of the subject under study rather than a practical application thereof. Applied research is directed toward practical applications of knowledge.* [6]

Basic research produces a greater understanding of phenomena, or the relationship between phenomena, and is not intended for practical utility. Applied research, however, yields plans, procedures, or policies for development, and is intended to have almost immediate utility. Although applied research focuses on general problem solving while evaluation research focuses on specific problem solving, evaluation research is considered a specific form of applied research, one whose primary objective is not the discovery of knowledge, but the testing of the applications of knowledge. Figure 4.2 represents the inherent

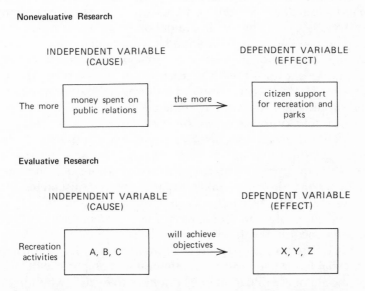

FIGURE 4.2 Nonevaluative and Evaluative Research Hypotheses

differences between nonevaluative (basic) and evaluative (applied) research hypotheses. Nonevaluative research usually may test a hypothesis concerning the relationship between the amount of money spent on public relations and the amount of citizen support for recreation and parks. Nonevaluative research tests the validity of this hypothesis and enlarges upon other intervening variables that may affect the relationship between money and support.

Evaluative research utilizes a similar logic: the dependent variable is the desired effect, while the cause or independent variable is the object of a planned recreation program. Just as the nonevaluative hypothesis requires further testing to eliminate or change the variable relationship, so too must the evaluative hypothesis be critically examined to test whether or not the activities really achieved the desired objectives and to explain how and why they did so.

Both nonevaluative and evaluative studies rely on research designs for data collection and scientific method for analysis. The validity of both study types is equal to the degree to which each follows the principles of scientific method.

Differences

Nonevaluative and evaluative research have a number of distinguishing characteristics. The distinction of *evaluation* versus *research* is in intent—that is, why each is done. It would appear that research and evaluation are done for different reasons. Research is undertaken largely to satisfy curiosity, while evaluation is done to solve a particular or specific problem and is intended for immediate use. A study to determine the relationship between an individual's amount of education and level of position in recreation and parks would be considered research. However, a study to determine whether a teen center recreation program successfully reduced the amount of juvenile vandalism of public property would be considered an evaluation.

Research and evaluation seek different ends and seek to answer different questions. Research seeks conclusions and the researcher provides the question. Evaluation leads to decisions and the question is asked by the decision maker rather than the researcher. In the examples above, the researcher is concerned with education level and type of position while the recreation board, commission, or administrator are concerned with juvenile vandalism.

Research attempts to explain the phenomena or relationship between variables, while evaluation attempts to compare "what is" with "what should be." Evaluation does not have to explain why a particular program is good or bad or how its objectives are being achieved. The primary purpose of evaluation is to measure program effectiveness against stated criteria or program objectives.

Evaluation in recreation attempts to measure a program's value and its social utility. Research, on the other hand, attempts to measure scientific truth, and if it yields evidence of social utility, it does so indirectly. Research is concerned with the production of knowledge, and its use is not of primary concern. Evaluation, however, maintains utility as its primary rationale and purpose.

Similarities

The similarities between research and evaluation are important considerations. Both utilize the tools of scientific inquiry including case studies, questionnaires, interviews, observation, content analysis, control and experimental groups, rating scales, attitude inventories, and a number of other methods.

Research and evaluation are concerned with studying, measuring, understanding, and describing the causal relationship between phenomena or other variables. No one, single type of research is best, be it basic research or evaluation research, nor is any method of research better than another, be it empirical, historical, or philosophical. Ultimately, the purpose of the study is the most important consideration in choice of research typology and methodology.

To argue whether basic research is superior to applied research is as spurious as arguing whether a degree in science is superior to a similar degree in arts. It should be kept in mind that the practice of recreation is an art based upon the applied science of social work, which in turn draws upon the science of psychology and sociology, and utilizes the abstract sciences of mathematics and logic.

SUMMARY

Evaluation research in recreation and parks is programmatic because its main concern is to assist staff in planning and modifying program activities to increase the potential achievement of program objectives. Such research may be formative or summative in design. Formative studies provide information to the agency staff that may suggest change or modification in program input. Summative studies provide more complete information on program effectiveness when measured against stated objectives. Together formative and summative evaluation studies provide decision makers with information necessary to choose among competing program alternatives.

It is essential that the evaluation study answer the questions: who, what, when, where, why, and how. The definition of the evaluation question(s) is crucial to reach a mutual understanding of exactly what is to be investigated. This understanding may be difficult to reach alone since program objectives may be either vague or unstated. In addition, recreation and park programs often accomplish more than the stated objectives.

There may be different expectations of the evaluation study depending upon the level of potential user within the organization. Study limitations should be made clear from the outset, and the type of information to be collected should be agreed upon prior to conducting the study.

The question of who should carry out the evaluation, whether it be accomplished by the agency staff or an outside evaluator will depend upon who is best able to conduct the study. It is desirable to use both in-house and outside evaluators, but the critical factor remains that no matter which group is used, the study must produce valid and reliable information.

REFERENCES

[1] Andre L. Knutson, "Evaluation for What?" *Proceedings of the Regional Institute on Neurologically Handicapping Conditions in Children.* Berkeley, University of California, June 18–23, 1961, p. 109.

[2] Michael Scriven, "The Methodology of Evaluation," *Perspectives of Curriculum Evaluation* (Chicago: Rand McNally, 1967), pp. 39–83.

[3] The *Journal of Leisure Research* is a quarterly research monograph jointly issued by the U.S. Department of the Interior, Heritage Conservation and Recreation Service, and the National Recreation and Park Association.

[4] Bernard G. Greenberg, and Berwyn F. Mattison, "The Whys and Wherefores of Program Evaluation," *Canadian Journal of Public Health,* vol. 46, (July 1955): 295–96.

[5] Jeanne Nienaber and Aaron Wildawsky, *The Budgeting and Evaluation of Federal Recreation Programs or Money Doesn't Grow on Trees* (New York: Basic Books, 1973), pp. 8–9.

[6] National Science Foundation, *Reviews of Data on Research and Development,* no. 17 (Washington, D.C.: The Foundation, 1960), p. 5.

5

TYPES OF EVALUATION RESEARCH

The earliest attempts to evaluate recreation and park programs centered around the concept of measurement. This process consisted of measuring the amount of some entity (recreation staff, facilities, equipment, participants, etc.) against a predetermined and agreed upon set of norms or standards, usually established by a consensus of practitioners. Although standards for recreation are considered to have emerged in the early twentieth century, their existence can be traced to feudal Great Britain. One of the earliest standards for recreation has been identified by Johnson. His research, reported in 1926, showed that:

> Two acres was an English standard for the size of a playground as early as the fourteenth century. In the reign of Richard II it was declared that "the Lord of the Manor may not be custom to plow or break up two acres of land lying near the church, because it was anciently granted for the recreation of the youth after evening services on every Lord's Day.[1]

EARLY HISTORY OF RECREATION AREAS

England

Definitive measurement of recreation space was proposed in England during the late 1800s. The Earl of Meath, founder of the Metropolitan Public Gardens Association, proposed in 1883 that "a public space for recreation should be within a quarter mile of everyone's door."[2] In 1891, Sir Robert Hunter calculated that each new town should be able to secure about 5 percent, or 1/20, of its area for public open spaces.[3] These statements would seem to indicate that the concepts of service radius and area percentage related to the provision of recreation resources had their origin in England, and not, as many believe, in the

United States. Furthermore, in regard to space for children's playgrounds, the London Board of Education proposed the following:

> . . . in 1891 it was first provided that the minimum size of a site (playground) should ordinarily be one quarter of an acre for every 250 children . . .[4]

Two years later, in 1893, the Department Committee of Playgrounds, London Board of Education, voted to add to the school law a provision that would allow 30 square feet of play space per child.[5] This regulation was to apply to all new public elementary schools built after 1893. It would appear that England deserves the distinction for originating not only recreation resource standards relating to area percentage and service radius, but also the total amount of physical space per pupil on playgrounds.

United States

Approximately seven years later in the United States, George A. Parker, superintendent of Keney Park in Hartford, Connecticut, chaired a committee appointed by the American Park and Outdoor Art Association.* The committee was charged with the responsibility for determining park areas for cities, based on population, income, and valuation. Mr. Parker read his committee's report before the 1901 Association Convention. The conclusions his committee reached had a profound and lasting effect upon the provision of space allocated for recreation resources. The report stated:

> . . . One twentieth of the city's area should be reserved for parks and squares. A playground should be allowed at least 300 feet square to every square mile, and in densely populated sections, more than one. Four other small squares should be allowed to the mile, of at least ½ an acre each. A thousand acres would then be divided as follows:
>
> 10 acres in playgrounds and squares
> 40 acres for large parks
> 100 acres in streets and alleys
> <u>5 acres in school grounds, etc.</u>
> 155 acres for public purposes
> 850 acres for private ownership
> Does 15.5 percent, seem a large proportion to give up to public uses? Yet one-third of the cities already exceed that amount, and it

---

* One of the earliest membership organizations in the United States concerned with municipal recreation and parks.

is probable that if 20 percent, one acre in five, is devoted to public use, it will go far towards preventing over-crowding and make the other four acres more valuable.

. . . From what light we have, it would seem as if there should not be less than one acre of park area to 200 population . . .

. . . It would seem from what has already been done, that one acre in twenty should be set apart for parks and squares, and arranged for before it is too costly, but only developed at the rate of one acre to 200 population . . .[6]

Much of the present planning for recreation development can be attributed to this report, especially in the concept of acreage-to-population ratio. Variations of this concept have evolved through the years, but available acreage-to-population density ratios have continued to remain a major planning criteria for the provision of recreation resources. For example, acreage-to-population ratios continue to be promulgated by such diverse agencies and organizations as the Bureau of Outdoor Recreation (now the Heritage Conservation and Recreation Service), American Institute of Planners, National Recreation and Park Association, and a host of states, counties, towns, and cities.

TWO TYPES OF RECREATION AREAS

The Playground

Prior to the twentieth century, the one recreation resource that received major attention was the children's playground. Various attempts to estimate the space needed for children's play in the school ranged from 30 square feet per child to 300 square feet.[7] In 1908, one recreation authority concerned with elementary schools in the United States estimated that school playgrounds had only 10 to 20 square feet per child, "except in the newest schools where 30 square feet was regarded as a suitable standard."[8] The concept that playgrounds were the exclusive domain of children can be seen in the reports of writers of the period who proposed standards for small children, as well as older children. Often, standards were further broken down to include provisions for both boys' and girls' play. Usually, playgrounds for small children and girls received a lesser space allocation than that for older boys.[9] Over the ensuing years, people began to realize that playgrounds were not the exclusive province of children, but that some provisions should be made for all ages. Today playgrounds often include such facilities as tennis courts and other active areas that can be used by adults and children.

Parks

Aside from children's playgrounds little thought had been given to other recreation resources until Henry Hubbard, a professor of landscape architecture at Harvard University, proposed a "system" of recreation resources at the 1914 National Conference on City Planning. He identified eight types of recreation resources that progressive cities should have: reservation, large park, small park, playfield, boys' outdoor gymnasium, girls' outdoor gymnasium, children's playground, and special facilities (swimming pools, skating rinks, etc.).[10] From this point on, there was a major effort to determine and allocate space requirements for these resources. The resources themselves were planned around the concept of the neighborhood, and five planning criteria were utilized by recreation authorities of the day:

1. Size of areas was given in square feet or acres, either total space or per population ratio.
2. The location was suggested next, usually with a fixed ratio of distance from the proposed user.
3. The third criterion related to the layout of the area, and more often than not contained suggested facilities therein.
4. Equipment that was usually provided in similar areas was suggested.
5. The final criterion was leadership—the number of adults who should be present when the area was operating.[11]

Hubbard's eight types of recreation resources were later modified to include play lots, recreation buildings, and other facilities. How were these planning criteria and resources to be assessed?

Comprehensive measurement, or standards-oriented approaches to program evaluation were proposed in 1951 by the National Recreation Association[12] in its publication, Schedule for the Appraisal of Community Recreation. This pamphlet detailed the sum total of recreation programs, structure, and resources for an "ideal" community; other communities were to measure themselves against this ideal. No attempt, however, was made to identify or explain what characteristics were inherent in this ideal community. This pamphlet was revised in 1959 by the Middle Atlantic District Advisory Committee of the National Recreation Association in its Guide for The Evaluation of Community Recreation, and again in 1965 by the Great Lakes District Program Standards Committee in Evaluation of Community Recreation: A Guide to Evaluation with Standards and Evaluative Criteria.

This measurement-oriented process still is the most widely used evaluation approach in recreation today. Primarily, this process is intended for internal or self-evaluation—departments or institutions are

judged on such evaluative criteria as: philosophy and goals, administration, personnel, programs, areas, facilities and equipment, and evaluation. Within this approach, standards are proposed for the amount
of office space for personnel, the amount of citizen participation in
the planning process, the amount of regular departmental operation
reports, and other criteria. Van der Smissen proposed that "The Standards and evaluative criteria apply to *all* public recreation and park
departments . . ."[13] Berryman's measurement approach, suggests
that such an instrument is essential because:

> *Agencies can use this instrument for self-study; to test new pro-*
> *grams; to indicate areas of the program that are most effective and*
> *areas where changes are needed to bring about more desirable*
> *outcomes; and to prove to a doubting public that the agency is*
> *carrying on the service in the manner that is described in its state-*
> *ment of aims and objectives . . . It is expected, as this tool is made*
> *generally available, that recreation services to disabled children and*
> *youth will be expanded and made more effective.*[14]

There are severe disadvantages however in using a measurement
evaluation approach for recreation and park programs. First, because
standards change, their duration is over a single time frame. Second,
this approach tends to obscure the fact that value judgments are
involved in setting standards, and unproved judgments reduce content
validity. Third, there is no empirical evidence that reliance on program
standards themselves will produce effective recreation programs.
Fourth, evaluation is limited to those criteria that can be easily measured. Other criteria that vary from community to community such as
education level, per-capita income, and other socioeconomic characteristics cannot be measured within this evaluation approach. Finally,
universal standards become ends in themselves and replace individual
program goals and objectives. Universal standards discourage individuality since nonadherence to standards is undesirable, and the standards approach, although possibly answering the question "Is the program effective?", neglects the other important question, "Why is it
effective?"

THE PROFESSIONAL JUDGMENT APPROACH

Another common evaluation approach in recreation and parks in direct
program observation by one or more experts who judge program
effectiveness. Often, these judgments are based upon comparisons

between similar and exemplary programs, at least in the view of the expert. An example of this approach is the National Recreation and Park Association's accreditation program to measure the effectiveness of college and university recreation curricula. Selected recreation educators and practitioners comprise visitation teams who visit and observe educational institutions' recreation curriculums. However, while evaluative criteria[15] do exist, they are generally not applied by the visitation team, but rather by the professional staff of the educational institution being visited. The rationale is that these staff members will better understand their programs as a result of this process of application. The judgment based upon experience, expertise, and accumulated data becomes the evaluation.

Another similar approach is the community recreation survey. Data is gatherd by an ad hoc group representing administrative and/or supervisory staff whose main concerns are program, facilities, and staff. The group studies the recreation resources for a relatively short period of time, gains its data mainly through impressionistic means, then evaluates. This judgment then, either positive or negative, becomes the evaluation.

Another judgment approach to evaluation is the oral examination required of doctoral students in recreation and park curriculums. The examination may be limited to the dissertation itself, or may range over the candidate's entire substantive field. Seldom is there any standard or uniform format with well-defined criteria with which to judge the quality of the candidate's responses. Ambiguity of objectives on the part of the candidate and the committee often make both the question and the response extremely vague. The final evaluation, the pooled reactions—often intuitive—of the committee, is made immediately after the candidate leaves the examining room. Again, this judgment is the evaluation.

Advantages of this approach are the ease of implementation and the immediacy of judgment. However, its disadvantages far outweigh its advantages. Most experts in recreation and parks would probably not rely on this approach if there was a viable alternative. The absence of other measures rather than convenience forces this approach. The reliability and objectivity of this approach are extremely questionable. Even if one were to concede the expertise of the evaluators involved, failure to apply the tenets of scientific inquiry causes one to doubt its validity. In addition, since experts often represent extremely diverse disciplines within the recreation and park field, it is often impossible to reach a consensus. The result is often compromise, which may not be in the best interest of the program or activity undergoing the evaluation.

THE NEED INDEX OR
SOCIOECONOMIC APPROACH

The concept of assessing need for recreation service is based upon the notion that individual and group differences do exist among community residents. Although the need process has been utilized as an approach to evaluation, it is also a planning process. The Community Council of Greater New York carried out a study to determine the social and economic differences among New York City neighborhoods, in an effort to assign priorities to those residents who had the greatest need for recreation resources. Two indexes were developed: (1) a neighborhood index of socioeconomic conditions based upon income level, juvenile delinquency rate, population, and ethnic composition; and (2), a neighborhood index of existing recreation services based upon participation patterns, existing facilities, and amount of leadership provided. The data obtained from the indexes were correlated and converted to a number for each neighborhood. A city-wide average was established and each neighborhood was compared with that average. Neighborhoods were then grouped into degrees of need based on five quartiles: very much above average need, above average need, average need, below average need, and very much below average need. The goal of this study was to develop a sound set of priorities to guide the planning and coordination of recreation services and resources.[16]

In 1966, the Recreation and Youth Services Planning Council of Los Angeles developed a similar procedure to establish priorities for the provision of recreation resources. A need index was derived from four population characteristics: population density, percentage of residents between the ages of 5 and 19, median family income, and juvenile delinquency rate. A resource index was then developed from existing park acreage in each of the city's 65 statistical areas. A priority schedule was determined by subtracting the resource index from the need index. The areas were then assigned a priority based upon four quartiles: need, high need, higher need, and highest need.[17]

The New York City Community Renewal Program instituted a study in 1968 that emphasized the assignment of budgetary priorities in capital expenditures for recreation resources within city neighborhoods. Median income of residents, city-wide average of facilities, and cost per user for proposed recreation resources were the need factors used. Neighborhoods were grouped into three areas of priority: first priority being given to "major action areas", second priority to "preventive renewal areas", and third priority to "sound areas."[18]

The major weakness in these recreation evaluation approaches is that no attempt is made to measure the overall effecitveness of the various programs; rather they merely statistically measure those neighborhoods that were above and below the city-wide averages. These studies initially attempted to equalize the amount of resources within the city by implementing a mathematical average. Later, socioeconomic data were added to the formula which pointed out graphically that certain areas within the city due to low income, high population density, and other factors had a greater need for resources than others. However, again the average basis was utilized, and no attempt was made to measure the effectiveness of the "average" area resources. Judgments were made solely on quantitative elements.

OTHER RECREATION
EVALUATION APPROACHES

The Los Angeles Recreation and Youth Services Planning Council undertook a study designed to develop a behavioral approach to evaluating the effectiveness of recreation programs in a school setting, through assessment of participant behavior. The council developed an instrument based upon a taxonomy of recreational behaviors that surveyed recreation participation patterns of junior-high-school students. However, the validity of the instrument could not be established and the conclusions suggested that the junior-high-school students self-report technique was unreliable since the research team found that these students could not accurately respond to the survey items.[19]

The Milwaukee Public Schools Division of Municipal Recreation and Adult Education has developed *A Handbook of Information: Program Evaluation* for its full-time personnel. At the end of each year program staff submit reports on activities, facilities, and staff which are then compiled into the *Handbook*. Quantitative data deals with program attendance, service statistics, and budget; qualitative data is obtained through participant interviews and questionnaires, staff observation, and employee conferences. However, the weakness of this evaluation approach lies in its adherence to arbitrary program standards and personal leadership traits. No attempt has been made to determine the validity or reliability of any of the evaluation report forms.

An approach that assesses the value of recreation programs, patterned after the congruence of goal-achievement models, has been proposed by Diana Dunn and Harry Hatry.[20] This approach attempts to measure such variables as attendance rates, facility and activity accessibility, use, appearance and variety, and socioeconomic data such as crime, delinquency rate, illness rate, and the state of the economy. The authors suggest a correlation between recreation programs and such diverse effects as a reduction in crime, maintenance of health, and a positive economic climate. Although such a relationship between variables is only tentative, recreation researchers have little or no evidence to support this theory. Empirical evidence correlating the effect of recreation programs on the community and on the individual is scarce.

Joseph Bannon's evaluation system for the delivery of leisure services suggests that the planning and evaluation processes proceed together since they are interdependent. Although agreeing that the essential purpose of evaluation is to determine whether or not a recreation program is achieving its objectives, Bannon recognizes that objectives are not immutable, and are subject to modification or change. Bannon proposes a two-track model (Figure 5.1)[21] that seeks ongoing evaluation information from the original planners, that is, the community citizens and the recreation staff.

Bannon suggests that citizens must be involved in the program on a continuing basis, not simply at the initial planning stage, in order to provide continuous feedback on the agency and its program. Although he suggests that this model also can be used to assess existing programs, it is difficult to accomplish since evaluation is in this case summative—,it is more easily accomplished at the end of the program or at the end of a track cycle. Evaluation should be an ongoing process and can be accomplished at any time during the program cycle. However, it is best done before the program begins operation (planning), but it can also be done while it is in operation (monitoring), or at its conclusion (outcome). The model is more valuable for evaluating a program that is the result of comprehensive planning than one that is already in operation. The most serious weakness in the model is in its final stage. Rather than an ongoing evaluation of the recreation program, Bannon suggests that there is a need to determine how often and under what conditions other evaluations must take place. He suggests that this varies with the type of activity being assessed. The evaluation model then becomes too closely tied with the planning process which suggests a periodic update on a three-to-five-year basis. In order to accurately measure effectiveness, and to be effective, program evaluation must be conducted on a continuous, uninterrupted basis.

A Total Evaluation Process (TEP) model for recreation and park evaluation has been proposed by Roger Mannell (Figure 5.2).[22] He suggests that there are a number of factors that influence program objectives and the activity program itself such as participants, the sponsoring agency, local government, and the mass media. When an assessment

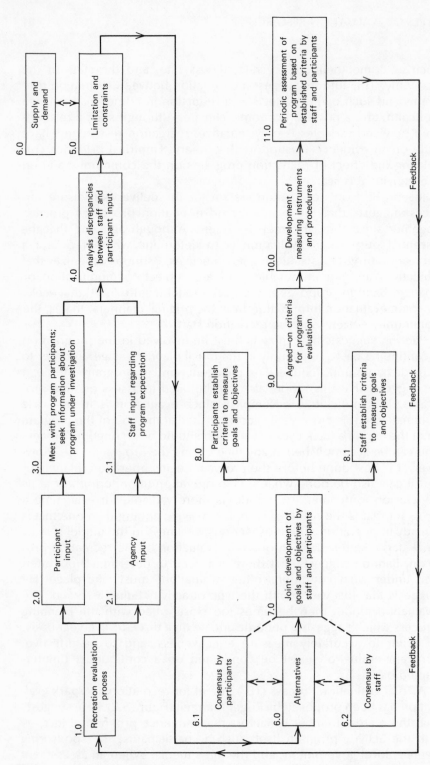

FIGURE 5.1 An Evaluation System for the Delivery of Leisure Services

SOURCE: Joseph J. Bannon, *Leisure Resources: Its Comprehensive Planning,* Copyright© 1976. Reprinted by permission of Prentice-Hall, Inc., Englewood Cliffs, New

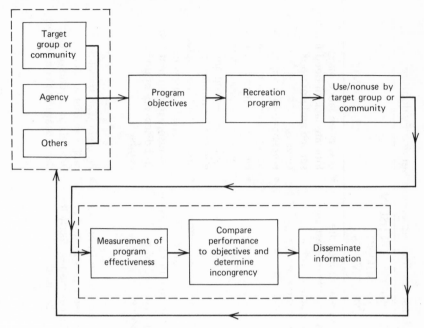

FIGURE 5.2 Total Evaluation Process

of the program has been completed, then its effectiveness can be compared against its stated objectives. The information obtained as a result of the assessment should be disseminated as widely as possible to the agency, to funding bodies, and to the community, by all possible means including workshops, clinics, news releases, and mailed report summaries. Essentially, the Mannell model is a discrepancy technique that measures promise against performance.

Mannell has also provided recreation and park administrators with a comparison and summary of program evaluation measures (Table 5.1).[23] This comparative summary suggests measures of program effectiveness, methods of data collection, assumptions for use in measuring program effectiveness, and comments on each technique. Evaluation measures include those proposed by Dunn and Hatry, Fisk, et al., McLean and Hermanson, van der Smissen, Siderelis, Bannon, and others who have proposed ratio measures of evaluation.

The final evaluation approach in leisure services is the Economic Equivalency Index (EEI) developed by Robert Wilder.[24] The EEI evaluation attempts to place a monetary value on a social service or good. It is predicated upon the concept that time is money, and therefore every working hour has value. It further assumes that this social value to the community (expressed in economic terms) is the equivalent of

TABLE 5.1 Summary of Suggested Effectiveness Measures for Recreation Service Evaluation

MEASURES OF PROGRAM EFFECTIVENESS	METHODS OF COLLECTION	ASSUMPTIONS FOR USE IN MEASURING EFFECTIVENESS	COMMENTS
1. Total *attendance* and *participant hours* (total time spent utilizing service) for each major activity or facility during a given time period. (Dunn and Hatry, 1971; Fisk, et al., 1973.)	• Registrations and admission fees. • Systematic sampling of programs at various times. • Surveys requiring user estimates.	• Assumed to indicate community interest and satisfaction with a recreation service.	• Low attendance may indicate lack of need for the service and not poor service. • Percentage of community using service not known. High attendance may not reflect high satisfaction but high need—program may need to be improved.
2. Number and percent of *different* participants and nonparticipants for each major recreation service during a given time period. (Dunn and Hatry, 1971; Fisk, et al., 1973.)	• Registrations and admission fees.	• Assumed to be a more specific indicator of who in the community is using and satisfied with a service.	• Coupled with demographic data allows groups or nonusers to be identified and discovery of unmet needs.
3. Number and percent of persons living within and beyond *so many minutes or miles* of a recreation service. (Dunn and Hatry, 1971; Fisk, et al., 1973.)	• Municipal population maps. • Public transportation schedules. • Citizen surveys. • Travel-time distance radius.	• Assume the further away a person lives from the service, the less likely it is to be used.	• Problem with travel-time radius in that artificial, natural, or psychological barriers are not considered.

Measure	Method	Assumptions	Notes
4. Crowdedness Indices: • Waiting times at facilities • Number turned away or deterred by crowdedness. • Ratio of capacity of service to usage. (Dunn and Hatry, 1971; Fisk, et al., 1973.)	• Sample waiting times at various times, seasons, days. • Citizen surveys. • Ask users if they *feel* the service is overcrowded.	• Assume overcrowded services decrease satisfaction with the service.	• Important not to look only at capacity measures but also at user perceptions of crowdedness.
5. *Variety* indices (number of different services available at various times. (Dunn and Hatry, 1971; Fisk, et al., 1973.)	• Simple count of number available. • Break count down for different client groups and areas in the community.	• Assumed a desirable quality in recreation. • Assumed to relate to satisfaction with recreation.	• Combine this information with #3.
6. *Safety* indices (number of accidents, injuries, criminal attacks, security). (Dunn and Hatry, 1971; Fisk, et al., 1973.)	• Most agencies have forms for recording this information as it occurs. • Usually expressed in number of incidents per a certain number of user days.	• Assume well managed and supervised services will have low rates of these incidents. • Assume high rates of these incidents will deter participants.	• Citizen survey can be used to determine percentage of nonusers avoiding services because "too dangerous."
7. Index of *physical attractiveness* of recreation areas and facilities. (Dunn and Hatry, 1971; Fisk, et al., 1973.)	• Citizen survey. • User ratings.	• Assume design, maintenance, and upkeep enhance recreation experiences and attract users.	• May wish to determine the number of potential users who stay away because of the facility used.

8. Index of *overall perceived recreation satisfaction* of citizens. (Dunn and Hatry, 1971; Fisk, et al., 1973.)	• Citizen survey (inclusion of a rating scale or scales to get a subjective judgment from users and nonusers.	• Perhaps one of the most important indicators. • Due to the subjective nature of this measure the way in which the information is obtained is very important. • No research is available to support this assumption • Indirect objective of recreation services. Often stated by proponents of recreation yet rarely evaluated.
9. *Delinquency and crime* indices (juvenile delinquency and crime rates affected by recreation programs). (Dunn and Hatry, 1971.)	• Information from the courts and police are available. • Break this information down by areas in which recreation services are available and relate to above measures. • Would require a special study.	• Assume that the perceptions by citizens will determine their behavior, i.e., they will become involved or not involved in service. • Assume that effective recreation services are useful in decreasing or controlling delinquency and crime.
10. Incidence of illness affected by recreation services. (Dunn and Hatry, 1971.)	• Would require a special study.	• Assumed that recreation services promote good physical health and psychological well-being. • Difficult to measure and is rarely if ever measured. • Often used as a rational for recreation services but rarely evaluated.
11. Economic impact indices (changes in business income, job opportunities, and property values affected by recreation	• Requires a special study.	• Unclear how this measure relates to recreation. • Difficult to measure and is rarely if ever measured.

Item	Methods	Assumptions / Questions
12. Hours of operation of programs and facilities. (Fisk et al., 1973.)	• Citizen survey. • User ratings.	• Assume that recreation services are more attractive at various times.
13. Helpfulness attitude of staff. (Fisk et al., 1973.)	• User rating.	• Assume that staff and user rapport increases satisfaction with service.
14. Cost or charge to users. (McLean and Hermanson, 1974.)	• Compare programs with fees versus programs without fees. • Ask users and nonusers how they feel about fees.	• Fees automatically limit population who may potentially use the service. • Does fee discriminate against certain segments of the population? • Does fee increase or decrease perceived user satisfaction with the service.
15. Self-evaluative check list with standards and evaluative criteria for recreation agencies, e.g., analysis of: a. philosophy and goals b. administration c. programming d. personnel e. areas, facilities, and equipment f. evaluation (van der Smissen, 1972.)	• Agency personnel. • Outside consultants. • Citizen boards or recreation commissions.	• Assume that an agency which meets all the criteria will be an effective one and meet the needs of the community. • No research to support this assumption. • Criteria tend to be vague. • May be useful as a guide for a department to determine the scope of their activity.

16. Organizational characteristics which predict recreation program effectiveness.
    a. need for community recreation services
    b. task orientation by recreation commission or board.
    c. recreation agency-municipality independency.
    d. supervisory competence.
    e. departmental size.
    f. mangerial style.
    g. organizational configuration. (Siderelis, 1976.)

• Interviews.
• Departmental records.
• Surveys and questionnaires.

• Assume that certain types of organizational characteristics are associated with more effective programs.

• Research support is meager for these assumptions.
• Further research is needed.

17.	Number and percentage of persons achieving instructional or skill objectives set for program e.g., swimming, weaving, etc. (Bannon, 1976.)	• Special tests of skills acquired.	• If a program is established to change attitudes or teach skills its effectiveness would be indicated by the number of participants successfully acquiring these.	• Suitable criteria for the number required to be successful for program effectiveness will depend on population and skills dealt with.
18.	Number of acres, areas, or type of facility per 1000 persons.	• Inventory of areas and facilities. • Number of persons in the community.	• Assumed that there is an optimal ratio for various services and that this will promote satisfaction with the service.	• Controversial as to what is a suitable criteria.
19.	Ratio of recreation staff to participants.	• Agency record.	• Assume that there is an optimal ratio which will promote satisfaction with the service and recreation experience.	• Controversial as to what is a suitable criteria.

that which a citizen would be willing to pay or give up for the recreation and park program. The proposed mathematical formula for the Economic Equivalency Index is PH × NP × MW ÷ AF = EEI. PH represents the number of hours of citizen participation. NP represents the number of participants in an activity. MW is the federal minimum wage standard (currently $2.65 per hour). AF stands for age factor; the authors distinguish between (1) adults, 19 years of age and above; (2) youth, ages 13 to 18; and (3) children, age 12 and under. For example, if there were 100 hours of participation in a recreation activity by 100 adults, and the minimum wage is $2.65 per hour, the Economic Equivalency Index for this activity would be $20,000. This dollar figure represents:

PH	NP	MW	AF	EEI
100 hours of	× 100	× $2.65	÷ 1	= $20,000
citizen	participants	minimum	adults	Economic
participation		wage		Equivalency
				Index

Wilder suggests that the EEI can be adjusted to take into consideration the type of individual participating in the program. If greater resources are necessary to provide services to special groups, a multiplier can be added to the equation. For instance, he proposes that senior citizens and the handicapped be given a multiple of 5, the economically deprived 4, and children and youth 3. If one chooses the previous example, the multiplier is added to the EEI, thus adjusting its cost upward:

PH	NP	MW	AF	EEI	Multiplier	adjusted
100	× 100	× $2.65	÷ 1	= $20,000 ×	5	= EEI
						$100,000

In this example, $100,000 would be the economic equivalency index for the leisure experience of the senior-citizen recreation program. The social value of this program to the community (expressed in economic terms) is assumed to be the equivalent of what its citizens would be willing to pay or to give up for this activity.

Wilder also suggests that the EEI could be used as a tool in program cost-benefit analysis. For example, if the adjusted EEI is $100,000, and the costs of the program, both direct and indirect are $50,000, then the fractional cost is $\frac{1}{2}$, and the decimal equivalent is 0.50. He proposed the possibility of imposing a policy that would eliminate a program or institute fees and charges to any activity that exceeds a 0.50 ratio.

This approach presents a number of difficulties. One of the most significant problems is to provide a logical and consistent rationale for placing a dollar figure on the worth of satisfying leisure experiences.

Nothing in the equation speaks to the point of individual differences in participants, either level, degree, or intensity of leisure experience. The formula presupposes that all participants share equally and uniformly in satisfaction derived from the activity. Although we have no tools to empirically measure satisfaction, we do recognize different outcomes within groups. In addition, if one were to use Wilder's EEI formula, small, new, or innovative programs that usually require high development costs might be eliminated in favor of mass programs with high attendance such as the traditional basketball leagues. If this situation were to occur, then the elevation of leisure services might as well revert back to assessment by compiling attendance records.

EVALUATION MODELS

The two conventional models or theories in the evaluation of programs are the goal-attainment model and the systems model. Since these models are widely used and are frequently referred to in literature, it is useful to describe the characteristics and limitations of each.

The goal-attainment model (see Figure 5.3) contains the intended outcomes or official goals of the program. It includes those processes that significantly influence program achievement. Related to this concept is the assumption that if specific program objectives can be defined, then the appropriate methodology and criteria for assessing the program will be selected correctly. The goal-attainment model is generally not concerned with implementation of findings. The evaluator's primary concern is with objectivity; the goals are accepted without question or modification. The evaluator has not helped develop the program's goals, and final evaluation may be based upon incorrect or

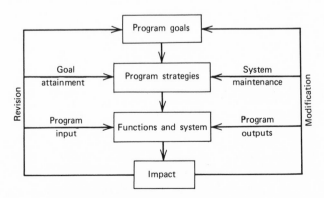

FIGURE 5.3 Goal-Attainment Model

inappropriate objectives. In addition, some organizational goals may in fact never have been intended to be realized. When this is the case, the administrator may see no need to modify the program to accommodate the research findings that the organization's goals are not being achieved. Finally, the goal-attainment model assumes that specific goals can be evaluated and modified apart from other goals sought by the organization. This assumption negates the fact that goals are interrelated by nature, and the modification of one goal is often constrained by the characteristics of others.

The systems model (see Figure 5.4) recognizes the fact that programs pursue other activities beside those directly related to official goal attainment. The systems model takes into account the competition between official goals and scarce resources. Some activities may be related to maintaining the system and may have no relation to official goal attainment. According to Schulberg, the systems model recognizes the organization's necessity to fulfill four main survival goals:

> . . . the achievement of goals and sub-goals; the effective coordination of organizational sub-units; the acquisition and maintenance of necessary resources; and the adaptation of the organization to the environment and to its own internal demands.[25]

The systems model focuses on the optimum distribution of resources and attempts to establish a working model to achieve organizational goals. In addition, it is concerned with the acquisition of new resources, maintaining the organization, adapting the organization to the environment, and molding it to fit internal demands. However,

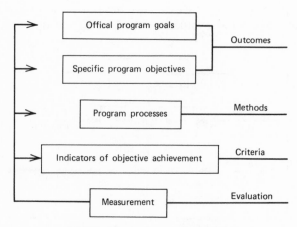

FIGURE 5.4 Systems Model

the systems model requires a great deal of knowledge and understanding of program activities. Because of these additional requirements, the systems model is both more demanding and more expensive. The demands for information necessary to understand the system, the scarcity of techniques for integrating this information, and the costs in terms of time and money, make the systems model impractical for all but a few recreation and park agencies.

In the final analysis, the evaluation problem will suggest the model to be used. If one is to measure only the extent to which a program achieves its goals, the goal-attainment model may be sufficient. If the question is more complex, and is concerned with the optimum distribution of resources among program components, the systems model may be more appropriate.

EXAMPLES OF GOAL-ATTAINMENT MODELS

A number of new approaches to program evaluation that utilize individual goal-attainment models have profound implications for evaluating therapeutic recreation programs. These approaches differ from traditional goal-attainment models in that they provide for goal setting as a regular program activity, while facilitating the assessment of program outcomes. Although these models focus on individual client goals and the extent to which they are attained, grouped together, they can be used also to evaluate programs. The models: (a) concrete goal setting, (b) goal-oriented automated progress note, (c) activity analysis, (d) goal-attainment scaling, and (e) patient progress record provide feedback mechanisms which can lead to program improvement, thus meeting one of the requisites of program evaluation.

Concrete Goal Setting

Upon admission to an institution or program an individual client record is begun containing client goals, staff members assigned, methods or procedures to be used in goal attainment, and the date for a periodic review of his progress is begun. (Figure 5.5) The information in this record can provide data on assessing progress in achieving client goal achievement, determining which methods or procedures are more effective, and if compared with other clients in the program, may indicate a preliminary measure of overall program effectiveness (see Figure 5.6 for an outline of concrete goal setting).

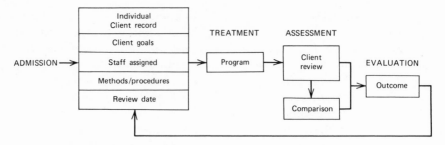

FIGURE 5.5   Concrete Goal Setting

Goal-Oriented Automated Progress Note

This approach (Figure 5.6) is primarily an attempt to describe the client's condition, establish realistic goals, and select the appropriate methods or procedures for achieving the established goals. Unlike the previous model, staff members select from a list of over 700 goal statements, those medical, symptomatic, ego-centered, interactional and discharge goals that are appropriate for the client. Two scales are appended to each goal, and, periodically, staff members indicate the importance of the goal for the client, and record client progress toward or away from this goal. Methods for individual goal achievement are recorded, and in addition to periodic client review, selected goals and methods are viewed in terms of their appropriateness for the client. Client evaluation consists of reviewing the total number of success scores against the goal statements for each client.

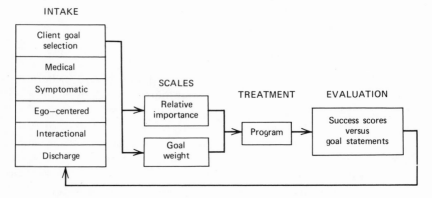

FIGURE 5.6   Goal-Oriented Automated Progress Note

Activity Analysis

Although primarily intended as a tool to aid in the selection of recreation activities to facilitate patient rehabilitation, activity analysis can help provide evaluation data (see Figure 5.7).[26] The client initially undergoes one or more social, psychological, and/or medical diagnoses. Treatment goals are then established in one of the behavioral domains. After the treatment plan is determined, the client's ability and skills are matched against one or more recreation activities that have been analyzed in terms of their component parts which are compatible with and appropriate to the treatment plan. The program is then begun, and at a prescribed period(s), an evaluation of client progress is made.

Goal Attainment Scaling

Upon admission, the client undergoes one or more interviews with program personnel who negotiate the number of goals to be attained. Each goal is assigned a relative weight and an initial score of goal attainment level or expected outcome is produced at the beginning of treatment. Upon completion of the treatment program, a second score is determined and the initial score is subtracted to yield a measure of client change. Change scores in all client activities are gathered, and using a formula specifically developed for this approach, program effectiveness can be measured against the expected client level of accomplishment (Figure 5.8 outlines goal-attainment scaling).

Patient Progress Record

Like goal attainment scaling, the patient progress record (Figure 5.9) establishes client goals at admission. A scale of values from 1 (most desir-

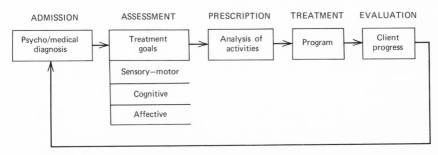

FIGURE 5.7   Activity Analysis

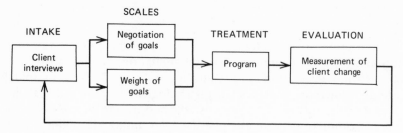

FIGURE 5.8   Goal-Attainment Scaling

able) to 7 (most undesirable) is derived for each client, and at periodic intervals, the program staff assesses client progress and determines the goal attainment level. Evaluation is accomplished by measuring the amount of client movement toward the most desirable values established at admission.

EXAMPLES OF SYSTEMS MODELS

A number of approaches to program evaluation that utilize management systems attempt to define goals and objectives more fully, and are concerned with the degree to which these goals and objectives are attained under certain circumstances. Although not "pure" evaluation models, these systems do provide information on the cost and benefit of competing goals or programs, which, in turn, enables decision makers to distribute resources on an optimum basis. Although systems approaches are more demanding and more expensive to operate than goal-attainment models, they do provide more consistent and meaningful data for making critical program decisions. A number of management systems approaches utilized today include: (a) Program Evaluation and Review Technique, (b) Critical Path Method, (c) Management By Objectives, and (d) Planning-Programming-Budgeting-System.

Program Evaluation and Review Technique (PERT)

The PERT approach was originally designed to assist planning and hasten the development time of the Polaris missile, a sea-to-air ballistic missile launched from a submarine, that has the capacity to seek out and destroy hostile aircraft. PERT is essentially a management tool whose task is to define and coordinate what must be done to successfully complete the objectives of a project, and to accomplish these *on time*. It attempts to both plan and control one-time projects—that is, jobs that have not been done before, nor will be done again in the same manner. Therefore, it becomes a scheduling technique that attempts to estimate the time it takes to complete a series of events, which leads ultimately to a project's completion.

Critical Path Method (CPM)

The CPM management system is similar to PERT in that it is also a scheduling technique, but unlike PERT which has no similar experience to guide it, CPM is used in projects where there has been previous experience, such as in construction. It is primarily a planning and control technique used in projects where past *cost* data are available. The system is concerned with obtaining the trade-off between the cost and completion date for large projects. It emphasizes the relationship between applying more workers or other resources to shorten the time of certain project jobs, and the increased cost of these additional resources.

In recreation and parks, the Program Evaluation and Review Technique could be used to develop master plans for open space and recreation activity. The Critical Path Method on the other hand can be used to determine the need for recreation resources such as swimming pools, recreation centers, and playgrounds. The major difference between PERT and CPM is that the former is used more in the research-and-design phase of a project, while the latter is mainly used in projects where there has been previous experience.

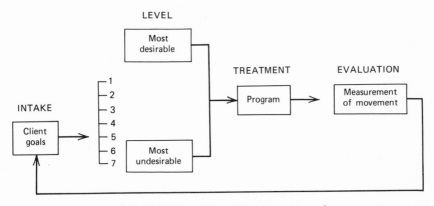

FIGURE 5.9 Patient Progress Record

Management by Objectives (MBO)

A time-consuming, but nevertheless effective, management system, MBO is primarily an appraisal of management performance. It begins by identifying organizational goals, then establishing procedures for distributing responsibilities among individual managers in order that their combined efforts are directed at achieving organizational goals. The process provides for the maintenance and growth of an organization by means of statements of what is expected of each individual involved in the process, and the measures of what is actually achieved. It assigns risks to all management personnel, and makes their progress—indeed even their tenure—dependent upon the results they produce. Management personnel identify and clarify organizational goals, define each member's major area of responsibility in terms of expected results, then establish individual member objectives. The process uses these measures as operating guides for each organizational unit, then monitors each member's objectives at prescribed periods. Finally, each member's performance is reviewed, and an assessment is made of the contribution of each member of the organization.

Only a few recreation and park departments are currently using this technique, and of those that are, the management team usually consists of the deputy or assistant administrator(s), the regional, activity or area supervisors and, recreation specialists or park supervisors. MBO has proven to be an effective management system in both the private and public sectors. However, it requires that the organization commit time, expense, and effort.

Planning-Programming-Budgeting System (PPBS)

Developed in the early 1960s by the U.S. Department of Defense, PPBS primarily is a planning mechanism that integrates information of all types into a single, coherent, management system. Like Management by Objectives, PPBS requires careful and precise development of organizational goals (while at the same time measuring the anticipated benefits against estimated costs). Budget requests are made in the context of a long-range program and budgetary plan. The process originates with a systematic analysis of alternatives which consist of:

1. Identification and description of agency objectives.
2. Projection of need to future years.
3. Explicit, systematic identification of alternative ways of reaching the objectives.
4. Estimate of total cost of each alternative.

5. Estimate of expected results of each alternative.
6. Determining the cost/benefit of trade-offs among alternatives.

PPBS is result oriented since the element of planning, when combined with the other objectives of control and management (budget and program), forces the system to review past activities and to formulate future policies within the context of organizational goals and objectives. This process allows choices to be made among competing alternatives for budgetary support.

For recreation and parks, PPBS may offer an alternative in identifying program goals and objectives, while providing necessary information on the costs of operating each activity. The difficulty however comes when these costs must be evaluated in terms of their effectiveness in meeting goals and objectives. It is far less complex to measure the cost-benefit of an economic product than it is a social action program such as recreation. Federal as well as local governments have in the past few years moved away from PPBS because of the difficulty in securing enough program information to provide for the evaluation phase of the system. Without such data on program effectiveness, as well as the time-consuming task of analyzing *all* competing alternatives, much of the budgeting and planning in government has returned to an incremental system for resource allocation.

ADDITIONAL EVALUATION APPROACHES

Recreation and park agencies must deliver services to their constituents. The result of these services are the *product* or program activities they conduct. Michael Scriven suggests that almost any product to which communication refers can be evaluated. He has proposed a five-point checklist, the Product Evaluation Profile (PEP): [27]

1. Need. Where it all begins—that is, a needs assessment should provide justification for program development. If the product (program) satisfies a genuine need or a defensible desire on the part of the consumer (participant), then a rationale exists for developing programs to meet these needs.
2. Market. If the agency had a program that in principle could meet the need, could they actually meet that need in practice? Planning is essential to determine the feasibility of the program and the odds for its achievement.
3. Data. What information does the program personnel have to know about the activity to decide whether in principle it meets the needs? Performance criteria are essential in order to assess ability to deliver against stated needs.

4. Performance. Does the program meet the need? Measurements must be taken to determine the effects and extent of the program's ability to meet identified needs.
5. Cost-Effectiveness. Has the program justified its cost, or more simply, was it worth it? All costs, both direct and indirect, must be calculated to determine value to the agency and to the participants.

A second evaluation approach proposed by Scriven, Goal Free Evaluation (GFE),[28] has been heavily criticized. An alternative approach to PEP, GFE measures the actual effects of a program against a profile of demonstrated needs. Its purpose is to accurately identify program effects in order to determine their quality and importance. Critics of this approach claim Scriven purposely ignores the goals and objectives of a program. Scriven proposes that by not seeing or knowing the goals, the evaluation is more likely to notice important side effects of the program. Essentially, unanticipated consequences of a program, rather than its intended effects are Scriven's major concern.

Scriven's earlier ideas of program evaluation are extended to a second checklist, the Pathway Comparison Model (PCM). This approach suggests that evaluation is essentially a data-gathering and data-reducing process that synthesizes information about programs in order to obtain an overall judgment of effectiveness. The checklist contains these nine steps:

1. Characterizing the nature of the program to be evaluated.
2. Clarifying the nature of the anticipated conclusion.
3. Assessing evidence about cause-and-effect relationships between independent and dependent variables in the program.
4. Comprehensively checking for all consequences of the program.
5. Determining and assessing the criteria of merit and the philosophical arguments pertaining to the program.
6. Assessing various kinds of program costs.
7. Identifying and assessing the program's critical competitors.
8. Identifying the program's constituents and performing a needs assessment to determine the program's potential impact.
9. Forming a conclusion about the merits of the program.[29]

Scriven suggests that the steps do not have to be taken in order, but they must all be completed before the PCM can be implemented. He suggests that the first six steps are formative evaluation measures, while the last three are summative measures.

The final approach to program evaluation is the Context, Input, Process, Product (CIPP) model proposed by Daniel Stufflebeam.[30] As indicated in Figure 5.10, this model divides administrative decisions into four classes: planning, structuring, implementing, and recycling.

In planning decisions there are a number of alternative objectives for the administrator to select. Structuring decisions are made when the administrator designs programs to achieve stated objectives. When the administrator is readly to operationalize and execute a program, decisions are implemented. Recycling decisions are made after judgments and reactions to program results.

Essentially, the CIPP model includes four types of evaluation since there are four different decisions to be made:

1. Context evaluation provides for planning decisions by helping to identify unmet needs. In addition, it helps determine unused opportunities and program problems.
2. Input evaluation facilitates structuring decisions by identifying and analyzing alternative program activities.
3. Process evaluation serves implementing decisions by monitoring the day-to-day program operation.
4. Product evaluation helps determine recycling decisions by identifying and measuring the results of the program.

CIPP program evaluation can also provide a basis for determining program accountability in addition to its decision-making function. For example, context evaluation records needs, opportunities, and objectives selected to meet these factors. Input evaluation provides information about program alternatives, while process evaluation provides data on how the program has been implemented. Finally, product

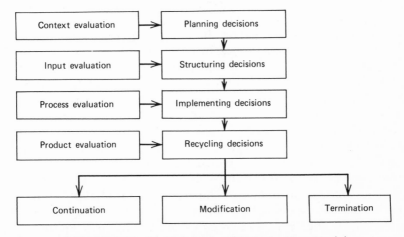

FIGURE 5.10 Stufflebeam's CIPP Evaluation Model

evaluation records the success or failure of the program, and provides information to decision makers with respect to its future operation.

Essentially, CIPP evaluations can be either formative or summative. If they are undertaken in order to serve decision making during program operation they are formative. Conversely, if they are conducted after the program has been completed, they are summative in design and serve the accountability function.

There are a number of differing models of program evaluation, many of which have been designed for a specific field or activity. It should be understood that evaluation models must be carefully chosen for their applicability and appropriateness to recreation and park programs, and often these models may require substantial modification in order to be effective. Differential evaluation may be a partial answer since individual activities are often perceived as being at different stages of development. Recreation program evaluation must seek to assess an activity at its present stage of development, so that the evaluation objectives and techniques are compatible with individual program objectives.

SUMMARY

Evaluation of recreation and park programs has traditionally consisted of counting the number of participants, comparing program efforts against predetermined standards of measurement, or utilizing the judgment of professionals within the field. Other approaches to program evaluation attempt to determine such factors as socioeconomic need, participant behavior, attractiveness and availability of facilities, and dependence upon planning.

Two conventional evaluation theories are goal-attainment and systems models. In the first theory, program effects are measured against intended outcomes, and the remaining discrepancy between these factors is the extent to which program objectives have been achieved. The latter theory focuses on the optimum distribution of resources and attempts to establish a working model to achieve organizational objectives.

Because of the unique individuality of recreation and park programs it must be understood that whichever evaluation model is chosen, "form should follow function,"—that is, the model selected should serve the individual needs of the user for information. Since user needs may be different from program to program, and since user needs may change over time, the design must be selected carefully in order to be appropriate, applicable, and usable.

REFERENCES

[1] George E. Johnson, "Play Space for Elementary School Children," *The Playground* **20** (October 1926):376.

[2] Basil Holmes, "Open Spaces, Gardens and Recreation Grounds." *Transactions of the Town Planning Conference, October 1910* (London: The Conference, 1911), pp. 483, 493.

[3] Ibid., p. 493.

[4] London Board of Education, *Report of the Departmental Committee Appointed to Inquiry into Certain Questions in Connection with the Playgrounds of Public Elementary Schools with Abstracts of Evidence,* (London, His Majesty's Stationery Office), 1912, p. 7.

[5] National Recreation Association. "Play Space for Schools," (New York: The Association) November 1938, p. 1. Mimeographed.

[6] American Park and Outdoor Art Association. "Report of Park Census for 1901," *Park and Cemetery and Landscape Gardening* **11** (August 1901):109.

[7] Jay B. Nash, *The Organization and Administration of Playgrounds and Recreation* (New York: A. S. Barnes and Co., 1927), p. 70.

[8] Jesse F. Steiner, *Americans at Play* (New York: McGraw-Hill Book Co., 1933), p. 21.

[9] London Board of Education. *The Playground Movement in America and Its Relation to Public Education,* Educational Pamphlet No. 27, (London, His Majesty's Stationery Office), 1913, p. 47.

[10] Henry V. Hubbard, *The Size and Distribution of Playgrounds and Similar Recreation,* n.p., *National Conference on City Planning* (August 1914):5–6.

[11] National Recreation Association. "Types of Municipal Recreation Areas," *The Playground* **30** (March 1937):595–98.

[12] In 1966, the National Recreation Association merged with a number of other professional recreation organizations to become the National Recreation and Park Association.

[13] Betty van der Smissen, *Evaluation and Self-Study of Public Recreation and Park Agencies: A Guide with Standards and Evaluative Criteria* (Arlington, Va.: National Recreation and Park Association, 1972), p. 5.

[14] Doris Berryman, *Recommended Standards with Evaluative Criteria for Recreation Services in Residential Institutions* (New York: New York University, School of Education, 1971), p. i.

[15] Council on Accreditation. *Standards and Evaluative Criteria for Recreation, Leisure Services and Resources Curricula Baccalaureate and Masters Degree Programs.* (Arlington, Va.: National Recreation and Park Association, 1975), 15 pp.

[16] Community Council of Greater New York, Research Department,

Comparative Recreation Needs and Services in New York Neighborhoods (New York: The Council, 1963), pp. 1–4, 123.

[17] Recreation and Youth Services Planning Council of Los Agneles, *"An Instrument for Determining Comparative Priority of Need for Neighborhood Recreation Services in the City of Los Agneles,* (Los Angeles, Cal.: The Council) September 1968, pp. 1–5. Mimeographed.

[18] City of New York, Community Renewal Program, *Recreation Facilities in New York City: A Method of Assigning Budgetary Priorities* (New York, City Planning Commission), November 1968, pp. 2–4.

[19] Recreation and Youth Services Planning Council of Los Angeles, *A Behavioral Approach to Evaluating the Effectiveness of Recreation and Youth Services Programs* (Los Angeles: The Council), September 1966, pp. 63–64.

[20] Diana Dunn and Harry Hatry, *Measuring the Effectiveness of Local Government Services—Recreation* (Washington, D.C.: Urban Institute, 1971). 47 p.

[21] Joseph J. Bannon, *Leisure Resources: Its Comprehensive Planning* (Englewood Cliffs, N.J.: Prentice-Hall, 1976), p. 281.

[22] Roger C. Mannell, "Evaluation Resources for Recreation Programs," Workshop Report (Wolfeville, Nova Scotia: Acadia University, Center for Leisure Studies, 1977), pp. 2–3 to 2–4.

[23] Ibid., pp. 3–1 to 3–6.

[24] Robert L. Wilder, "EEI: A Survival Tool," *Parks and Recreation* **12**:8 (August 1977):22–24, 50–51.

[25] Herbert C. Schulberg and Frank Baker, "Program Evaluation Models and the Implementation of Research Findings," *American Journal of Public Health* **58**:7 (July 1968):1252.

[26] For a more comprehensive treatment of activity analysis see Elliott M. Avedon, *Therapeutic Recreation Service: An Applied Behavioral Science Approach* (Englewood Cliffs, N.J.: Prentice-Hall, 1974).

[27] Michael Scriven, "Evaluation Perspectives and Procedures," in W. James Popham, ed., *Evaluation in Education: Current Applications* (Berkeley, Cal.: McCutchan Publishing Corp., 1974), pp. 291–33.

[28] Ibid., pp. 34–67.

[29] Daniel L. Stufflebeam, "Self-Study of Approaches to Evaluation," in Popham, ed., *Evaluation in Education: Current Applications,* pp. 116–142.

[30] For a more complete description of the CIPP evaluation model see Daniel L. Stufflebeam, et al., *Educational Evaluation and Decision Making* (Itasca, Ill.: F. E. Peacock Publishers, 1971).

6

DESIGN OF EVALUATION RESEARCH

One of the most vexing problems faced by recreation and park administrators is the need to evaluate leisure activity programs even
though procedures for conducting a scientific assessment are not
readily available. Program administrators are frequently so involved
with the day-to-day program operation that they simply cannot conduct an evaluation. This failure to determine whether or not program
objectives are being achieved often stems from the failure to recognize
what are the basic elements that constitute the activity program, or
the evaluation design.

Evaluation of recreation and park programs may be designed to
produce information about *effort, effectiveness, and efficiency* in
achieving the program's objectives. From this perspective, comprehensive evaluation of recreation and park programs includes an analysis of the input (effort), output (effectiveness), and cost-benefit (efficiency) ratio of individual activities or overall programs.[1]

ANALYSIS OF PROGRAM EFFECTIVENESS

Input

Program effort refers to the type, kind, and number of activities considered necessary to meet program objectives. It would include, but
not be limited to, such resources as staff, facilities, equipment, and
budget. In a program analysis the quantitative and descriptive information indicates an agency's commitment in terms of staff and ongoing program activities. This analysis does not assess such qualitative
aspects as how well the activity is being accomplished, or how well
the program objectives are being attained. Because recreation administrators often are concerned primarily with efforts, evaluation results
yield subjective, superficial, impractical information. However, if little
effort is invested in a program, there can be little hope for accomplish-

ment. Evidence of program activity alone is not sufficient to indicate objective attainment, and this single-dimension approach is extremely limited unless it also combines information on program effectiveness and efficiency.

Output

Program effectiveness refers to the extent to which the objectives of the program have been achieved. It is essentially an analysis of the difference between what was intended to happen and what actually did occur. The primary element is the measure of objective attainment. However, this measurement must also consider unanticipated consequences, both desirable and undesirable. Unanticipated consequences of a recreation program could include impaired participant experience should an activity be oversubscribed, and, conversely, a heightened participant experience if an activity planned to accommodate 25 people attracted only half that number. In an instructional tennis program, the first group would most likely receive far less individual attention than the second group.

Cost-Benefit Ratio

Program efficiency, the assessment of relative costs in achieving program objectives, compares the ratio of effectiveness-to-effort in terms of money, time, staff, facilities, and equipment. The effectiveness-effort comparison is based upon the extent to which objectives are achieved when measured against the type, kind, and number of resources considered necessary to achieve program objectives. Program efficiency assessments should answer the following questions: How economically does the program achieve its objectives? Can other programs achieve the same results at lower costs? How can the program be modified to make it more effective, while not increasing its cost?

Several cost-benefit, cost-effectiveness,[2] and other input-output approaches to program evaluation have been proposed in recent years. Proponents of the organizational theory approach to public recreation see this type of systems or operations analysis as the "wave of the future." In contrast, others feel that public recreation programs have their primary justification in human and social values, and not exclusively in economic terms. For example, a commercial amusement park may be assessed in terms of its net profit. However, it is quite different to assess the behavioral benefits of a public park. This latter resource must be viewed in social, not economic, terms. In addition, the individuals who derive the benefits of both resources will be quite different. In either approach the origin depends upon the development of clear, specific, and measurable program objectives.

CONCEPTUALIZING GOALS AND OBJECTIVES

Recreators as well as the general public want leisure-service delivery systems to provide the best possible programs at the least possible cost. The public is generally unconcerned how this is accomplished, so long as it is accomplished. Recreators, however, must deal constantly with how to provide the best possible program activities. One constant factor is that recreators will disagree. Some recreators argue for continually supervised programs, while others insist that self-directed activity is the best approach. Although recreators disagree on the best approach, most agree that recreation activities should be based upon sound program goals and objectives.

Chapter 2 distinguishes between goals and objectives. Goals were defined as ends to which a design trends; an ideal and a value to be sought after, not an object to be attained; a universal, a statement of highly desirable conditions toward which a society should be directed. Objectives, on the other hand, were defined as statements which were capable of both attainment and measurement. They are an aim or end of action, a point to be reached; a variable, the stated purposes of an organization or an individual, capable of planning and taking action to gain intended ends. Goals are ideals or values, and as such they cannot be attained. Objectives, on the other hand, can be attained, and in addition they can be measured. Failure to distinguish between goals and objectives is a problem in the program planning stage. Too often recreators propose goal statements, but do not suggest objectives. Or, the goals may be vague, ambiguous, and universal.

Typically, recreation and park department annual reports suggest purposes or goals in statements like:

1. To enhance the quality of life.
2. To provide a balance between humans and the environment.
3. To meet the needs and interests of citizens.

Not only are these goal statements impossible to achieve, but there is not universal agreement on what these statements actually mean. Such broad and nonsubstantive goals can be neither attained nor measured. Another example of goals that relate to individuals in recreation is the theory that:

For individualized programming, each program or activity should be designed to enhance or satisfy one or more of the following human

*needs: growth, maturation, both physical and psychological; phys-
ical fitness, skill and talent development for leisure enjoyment,
awareness, or exploration; opportunities for sports, both popular
and unusual; character building; reducing personal, family, group,
or community tensions; strengthening interpersonal relationships
and identities (family, group, and community); emotional stability;
peer group acceptance; sense of worth or achievement (individual
and communal); sense of belonging; positive channeling of asocial
behavior into community-accepted endeavors; community activity
and involvement to ensure safe streets, to stimulate perceptions, to
channel volunteers, and to meet individual or family crises.*[3]

All of these statements are appropriate to social action recreation
programs, but they cannot be universally attained, and some of these
individual goals are more important than others in different programs.
Goal priorities should be distinguished, and goal statements should
be translated into meaningful experiences (objectives) so recreation
and park departments can assess program effectiveness.

OBJECTIVES IN RECREATION
PROGRAM EVALUATION

A program objective is simply a written or expressed *intention* about
an intended outcome. Program objectives can be quite general or
specific, but they must be precise so that any activity or behavior is
measurable. In either case, program objective statements are essential
to the growth and development of recreation and park programs.
Behavioral objectives state potential changes in participants as a result
of the recreation program. Basically, an objective is a statement of
what the program should actually accomplish. For example, the stated
goal: "Making children safe while in, on, or about the water" may
be translated to the specific objective. "Each third-grade school child
will successfully complete the Red Cross Beginner Swimming Program." Once leaders and administrators of recreation programs know
what their specific objectives are, they have a foundation on which to
base a number of important decisions. They can select from a vast
array of activities those that can definitely help achieve objectives.
They can select equipment, facilities, and staff that will allow the
greatest potential for objective achievement. Objectives, then, provide
the basis for deciding what resources are necessary for particular
programs. In the previous example of the swimming program, if there
are 5000 third-grade children who cannot swim, then it is relatively
easy for program administrators to determine how many swimming

pools, instructors, and other staff and equipment are necessary to accomplish the specific objective.

Programs with no clearly defined objectives, are impossible to evaluate, and there is no logical basis for resource allocation. A carpenter selects a tool after he or she knows exactly what is to be built. Similarly, someone building a model airplane does not select materials until the blueprints (objectives) are read. Too often, however, recreation program planners initiate activities without every specifying what it is they hope to accomplish by these activities. Recreation program objectives provide planners and leaders with a sense of purpose and a focus for the program's direction.

As mentioned earlier, evaluation studies must provide information so decision makers can judge program alternatives. If the alternatives are a number of different activities, decision makers would like to judge the success of each, but in order to accomplish this they must first have a definition of success. Recreation program objectives provide this definition since they state what the activity is to accomplish. When objectives have been established, an evaluator only has to gather data to determine whether or not a particular activity is successful. Evaluating recreation programs without first knowing what the objectives are is as futile as trying to determine if someone has been successful in life without knowing what success means to that person.

It is important to distinguish between program objectives and program descriptions. For example, a description of a tennis instructional program tells you something about the content and procedures of the activity. A program objective, on the other hand, describes the desired outcome of the tennis activity. Both are important components in a recreation program, but recreators must realize that although a description often tells a great deal about what is contained in the activity, it does not provide a statement of intended outcomes. More importantly, it does not suggest how to know when the intended outcomes have been achieved. Although activity descriptions are helpful in planning recreation programs, the essential element remains the program objectives.

GENERAL VERSUS SPECIFIC OBJECTIVES

Any program objective must be clear, specific, and measurable. There are four distinct parts to a well written objective: it is stated in terms of the person, group, or thing that is to occur; it specifies a phenomenon or behavior that can be counted, verified, or measured; it specifies the conditions under which the phenomenon or behavior must occur; and it specifies a minimum level of accomplishment or performance. Thus, evaluation of recreation and park programs must measure the changes in phenomena or behavior that take place during activity. This does not mean that all the phenomena or behavior that occurs as a result of recreation programs can be measured by achievement tests. It does mean that the expectation of change implies varying degrees of behavior or actions, and this in turn can be measured. However, in recreation and parks today there are very few valid and reliable methods for measuring change.

If, for example, we wish to improve a senior citizen's aesthetic sense, and if he or she wants this improvement, then we must assume that aesthetic sense can be changed through some program of recreation activity. The classical technique would suggest measurement of the aesthetic sense both before and after the recreation program. But how does one measure asesthetic sense? Since it is probably impossible for any two people to agree on a definition of the concept of aesthetic sense, subjective judgments are used to determine any change in aesthetic sense. In a different physical recreation activity such as swimming, there are precise and universally accepted techniques to measure a participant's ability to swim 25 meters in less than two minutes.

General Objectives

Recreation administrators are generally concerned not with *specific* action or behavior in an activity, but rather with *general* action or behavior that results from recreation activity. A general objective like "to enhance the quality of urban life" may be universally accepted in the recreation field, but it does not have a universally accepted definition. Few people would disagree with the intent of this worthy objective. The added dimension of change (enhance) implies that quality of life can be measured. However, "quality of life" is not limited to a single, precise application, but quality is associated with a number of given activities. Since we do not know from the objective what behavior is to be observed, it is impossible to develop appropriate measurement procedures.

Another general objective for recreation might be that "participants' attitudes toward democracy should improve." Again, there is no concrete or specific application to be delineated. Like "the quality of life" objective, this objective, although abstract implies that behavior can be measured since it indicates that some improvement should take place. However, the evaluator cannot hope to develop an instrument for measuring improvement since the objective lacks the definition of the precise behavior to be observed.

If general objectives cannot be measured, what is their purpose? Probably the best rationale for stating objectives in a general manner is that people who prepare them need not be experts or specialists in recreation. General objectives afford individuals the opportunity to express their concern about the outcomes of a recreation program in a nontechnical manner. Community residents, politicians, board and commission members can express their program desires and leave the program process to trained recreation professionals. Once the public has expressed their general desires, recreation personnel can adapt and implement specific strategies to meet those objectives. General objectives do have a place in organized recreation programs even though they create problems for measurement. A recreation board or commission can develop general objectives for the entire department without limiting the objectives to a precise application. Similarly, a recreation director can establish general objectives for a community center without limiting the individual recreation leader's freedom to work toward these objectives through the development of specific programs. General objectives are meaningful to a recreation department and they should not be overlooked or discarded simply because they create measurement problems in the evaluation process.

Specific Objectives

Statements that are limited to precise applications and succeed in communicating the writer's intent are specific objectives. They focus on a specific group, a specific behavior, and a specific action. Interpretations of specific objectives usually are not subjective or variable. Specific objectives are derived from general objectives in that they allow the recreator to delineate general objectives as meaningful recreation outcomes that are both important and measurable. How do we move from general to specific objectives?

The general objective "to enhance the quality of urban life" is a statement of intent that might generate the following specific objective: "at the end of the recreation activity program, all the participants will be able to identify the architectural style of designated historic buildings within the city." This specific objective is measurable.

The general objective "participants' attitudes toward democracy should improve" might be extended to the specific objective: "at the end of a team flag-football program, all the participants will have been chosen as captain of their football team at least once." In behavioral terms, this specific objective can be measured through observation and recording.

The sequence of the goal-objective continuum should begin with the statement of a goal or direction in which a recreation and park department wishes to move toward. Then, general objectives should be stated to further narrow the focus of the department's direction. The specific objective is then stated, in terms of four basic elements:

1. The program or audience that is expected to perform.
2. The activity or participant behavior expected when performing.
3. The conditions under which the activity or participant will perform during the evaluation process.
4. The degree or point at which the activity or participant proves mastery of the objective.

Writing a specific objective, is similar to sentence structure: Who is to do something relates to the subject of the sentence; what is to be done relates to the sentence verb; what was done relates to the sentence object; and how is it to be done relates to the modifier in the sentence.

Vague goals and general objectives lead to vague or general conclusions which cannot be measured empirically. To reach definitive conclusions, goals and general objectives must be clear, specific, and related to concrete behavior that can be observed, recorded, and measured. Without such measurement, conclusions are subjective rather than objective.

Behavioral Objectives

With respect to behavioral objectives in recreation, municipal authorities generally do not expend energies in dealing with individuals as do those in therapeutic recreation programs.[4] Treatment goals for clients or patients are often prescriptive, and client progress is assessed on a periodic basis. Specific behavioral objectives deal with four common elements: audience, behavior, condition, and degree.

The more explicit the definition of audience, the more explicit is the specific objective, and the less the chance for confusion regarding whom the objective was designed for. Note the difference between the following audiences:

1. The children will construct a house from the eight wooden building blocks provided.
2. The cerebral-palsied children in the small muscle-hand unit of the hospital will construct a house from the eight wooden building blocks provided.

In the first example, it is not clear which children we want to construct the house. The second example more specifically defines the audience.

A description of the client's expected behavior during the performance is the core of the objective. Again, note the difference in the following two examples:

1. The client will understand the principle parts of a painting.
2. Each client in the fine-arts class will be able to identify the six principle parts of a painting, as defined by their workbook.

Again, the second example further identifies the specific audience, and the client and recreation leader know specifically what the expected behavior is. In the first example, neither the client nor the recreation leader share common knowledge of what is to be done. When objects are combined with verbs, the client and the recreation leader have more precise statements about what is to be done. However, it is important to use clear and unambiguous words to describe objectives.

Word Differences

Robert Mager offers a number of typically ambiguous words, then proposes others that are open to fewer interpretations.[5]

WORDS OPEN TO MANY INTERPRETATIONS	WORDS OPEN TO FEWER INTERPRETATIONS
to know	to write
to understand	to recite
to really understand	to identify
to appreciate	to differentiate
to fully appreciate	to solve
to grasp the significance of	to construct
to enjoy	to list
to believe	to compare
to have faith in	to contrast

SOURCE: From the book, *Preparing Instructional Objectives,* 2nd ed., by Robert F. Mager, Copyright© 1975 by Fearon Publishers, Inc. Reprinted by permission of Fearon-Pitman Publishers, Inc.

Many recreational goals and general objectives are too vague, abstract, or global to be evaluated objectively. Platitudes and other well intentioned but nevertheless intangible statements must be reduced to specific, observable behaviors. One goal may require several specific objectives in order to make its implications explicit. Specific objectives tend to be more definitive than goals since they must provide greater detail in observing behavior or activity. When writing specific behavioral objectives, a specialized verb must be used to limited interpretation. Such verbs as write, describe, name, identify, predict, infer, select, state, demonstrate, construct, build, estimate, measure, compare, distinguish, classify, support, accept, adopt, learn, visit, and persist are action verbs which usually correspond with specific objectives.

Norman Gronlund's list[6] of selected verbs for specific learning outcomes in school settings can be adapted for use in recreation programs.

1. **Creative behaviors**

Change	Modify	Paraphrase	Rearrange
Restructure	Retail	Synthesize	Vary

2. **Music behaviors**

Blow	Clap	Harmonize	Play
Pluck	Practice	Sing	Strum

3. **Arts behaviors**

Assemble	Color	Draw	Frame
Mold	Paste	Sculpt	Varnish

4. **Drama behaviors**

Act	Direct	Display	Emit
Express	Move	Respond	Show

5. **Complex, logical, judgmental behaviors**

Analyze	Contrast	Criticize	Decide
Defend	Explain	Generate	Structure

6. **Language behaviors**

Abbreviate	Capitalize	Edit	Outline
Pronounce	Read	Summarize	Write

7. **Mathematical behaviors**

Add	Compute	Count	Derive
Extrapolate	Graph	Reduce	Solve

8. **Laboratory science behaviors**

Calibrate	Conduct	Convert	Demonstrate
Grow	Manipulate	Prepare	Weigh

9. **Physical behaviors**

Bend	Carry	Float	Hit
Lift	Run	Ski	Throw

Classification of Objectives

Most written objectives in recreation, as in education, fall into three major learning domains or classifications: cognitive, affective, and

SOURCE: Reprinted with permission of Macmillan Publishing Co., Inc., from *Stating Behavioral Objectives for Classroom Instruction*, Copyright© by Norman E. Gronlund, 1970.

psychomotor. The following definitions are taken from Krathwohl, Bloom, and Masia:

Cognitive learning domain objectives emphasize remembering or reproducing something which has presumably been learned, as well as solving some intellectual task for which the individual has to determine the essential problem and then reorder given material or combine it with ideas, methods, or procedures previously learned. Cognitive objectives vary from simple recall of material learned to highly original and creative ways of combining and synthesizing new ideas and materials.

Affective learning domain objectives emphasize a feeling tone, an emotion, or a degree of acceptance or rejection. Affective objectives vary from simple attention to selected phenomena to complex but internally consistent qualities of character and conscience.

Psychomotor learning domain objectives emphasize some muscular or motor skill, some manipulation of material and objects, or some act which requires neuromuscular coordination. [7]

Cognitive objectives emphasize *thinking,* affective objectives emphasize *feeling,* and psychomotor objectives emphasize *acting.* It is well to realize that all objectives usually overlap each learning domain. The critical element to remember, however, is the primary emphasis of the objective. What behavior is emphasized in the objective? Is thinking, feeling, or acting the dominant behavior? Examples of the cognitive, affective, and psychomotor objectives applied to recreation programs might include:

Sample cognitive objective:
- A. Participants in a nature study activity.
- B. Will identify trees as being maple, oak, pine, or elm.
- C. When shown actual trees or pictures of them.
- D. They should be able to correctly identify 75 percent of the examples.

Since being able to identify different types of trees requires the participant to understand or comprehend the categories indicated, this is a cognitive objective.

Sample affective objective:
- A. Senior citizens in a music appreciation activity.
- B. Will demonstrate an increased interest in music by coming to class early.
- C. The recreation leader will have the room open so they may

come in early, but will not provide any special incentive for participants who do so.

D. The objective will be considered accomplished if an average of one-third of the participants come early throughout the program, and 75 percent come early at least once.

This objective suggests that a participant will feel more positive about music. Because learned interest rather than knowledge of the subject is the behavior involved, this is an affective objective.

Sample psychomotor objective:
A. Six-year-olds beginning a drawing activity.
B. Will draw.
C. A circle, square, and triangle using visual symbols.
D. Each symbol will be well-formed and created with a single, unbroken line.

Being able to draw symbols requires the participant to manipulate a pencil or pen to produce a product—hence this is a psychomotor objective.

In summary, cognitive objectives deal with what a participant should know, understand, or comprehend (critique a poem, spell a word, or solve a riddle). Affective objectives deal with how a participant should feel about something (appreciate literature, contemplate art, or enjoy music). Psychomotor objectives are concerned with how a participant controls or moves his or her body (serve a tennis ball, paint a picture, or do a square dance).

To write specific behavioral objectives Robert Mager suggests these three guidelines:

> First, identify the terminal behavior by name; you can specify the kind of behavior that will be accepted as evidence that the learner has achieved the objective.
>
> Second, try to define the desired behavior further by describing the important conditions under which the behavior will be expected to occur.
>
> Third, specify the criteria of acceptable performance by describing how well the learner must perform to be considered acceptable.[8]

Although it is not necessary to include all three guidelines in a written behavioral objective, use of all provides greater specificity, which, in turn, enables better communication between those involved in objective setting. A number of recreators may object that writing behavioral objectives takes time, effort, and practice. However, the recreation profession has been extremely lax in making its objectives specific, meaningful, and visible. Behavioral objectives provide a balance between subjectivity of values and objectivity of facts. Specific behavioral objectives can encourage better management, more effective program procedures, and a greater sense of public accountability. Once program objectives are agreed upon, the next step in the evaluation process is to formulate specific questions and measure the answers to those questions.

FORMULATING THE QUESTIONS

In program evaluation, typical questions that attempt to measure program effectiveness are:

1. To what extent is the program successful in reaching its objectives?
2. Is one activity more effective than another activity in attaining common objectives?
3. How well is the program faring in getting the desired results?
4. Which activities within the program are more effective than others?

Whatever questions are posed in the evaluation, the basic premise is the same: The program process is based upon the notion that there are goals and objectives, there is a planned program activity aimed at achieving those objectives, and there is some measurement of how well the objectives are being attained. Control variables are established to make certain that no external factor—such as a change in leadership or a reallocation of resources—was responsible for objective achievements.

After the specific program objectives have been selected for study and the evaluation questions have been posed, the next step is to develop indicators or instruments to measure the extent to which the program objectives have been attained.

MEASUREMENT

The initial task of the evaluator must be to examine existing records and other readily available information to gain some direction for the planning of the evaluation methodology. It may contain data such as expenditures, participation rates, leadership allocation, other statistical information, or even the results of other relevant reports or studies. Unfortunately, in the case of recreation and park programs, the initial examination of records may prove useless since recorded program information is often inadequate, irrelevant to evaluation, or unable to lend itself to systematic analysis.

Electronic Data Processing

The use of computers for information-gathering purposes is gaining considerable favor in some recreation and park departments. Electronic data processing currently is being used in payroll, inventory, and budgeting applications. However, recreation and park authorities generally give little attention to recording management information about socioeconomic and other data on program participants and to the plotting of demographic characteristics that could greatly enhance their programs.

An MIS (Management Information System) for a parks and recreation department should have the potential to provide significant economic, administrative, and social benefits. It should provide information about the operations of the department, about the recreation needs of the community, and about the implications of various decisions . . . This can be accomplished by integrating attendance and facility use data with other data, such as that gathered from citizen surveys and records of existing recreation opportunities, from both the public and private sector . . .[9]

A final example of computer usage that holds tremendous promise is *simulation*—the modeling of physical situations. For example, suppose a city's recreation facilities were overcrowded. Would modifying the hours of operation make the situation better or worse? One way to answer this question would be for the city to try the plan for a period of time to see what happens. However, this approach might be expensive, potentially frustrating to participants, and perhaps dangerous to decision makers. An alternative is to design a computer model of participation patterns that can provide the answer and allow experimentation without disturbing participants or city officials. A computer program can be written to describe the physical characteristics of the facilities, the participation rate at each facility, and the carrying capacity of each. The program then simulates the flow of participants into and out of the facility, keeping track of average numbers, overcrowding, and even the duration of individual participation. The program can simulate inclement weather and traffic hazards, and the researcher can observe the resulting facility use. In summary, the computer can do everything or more than an actual try-out would do, but the computer works faster, is less expensive, and has a much greater capacity for manipulation of critical variables.

Record keeping for evaluative purposes is slightly more difficult than most record keeping. What should be recorded must be related to each individual activity, but, as a general rule, one must look particularly to information that will help measure the extent to which a program achieves its objectives. Maintaining appropriate records for evaluation purposes achieves nothing in itself. What it does provide is user and resource information for planning and developing current and future programs.

THE PROGRAM SEQUENCE

Recreation program objectives are based on changes in individuals or groups. These changes can be in attitudes, behavior, or skills; they can be classified as physical or mental changes. It is recognized, however, that these changes can only be brought about under certain conditions. A successful program leads to achieving the desired objectives. Edward Suchman suggests one of two reasons for an unsuccessful program.[10] Either the program itself did not initiate the process necessary to achieve the objective (program failure), or the program did initiate this process, but the process did not yield the desired effects (theory failure). A modification of Carol Weiss's conceptualization of the two types of program failure is presented in Figure 6.1.[11]

In the first example, the program sequence is completed, since the recreation program produced the desired outcome. With theory failure, the recreation program also causes something to happen, but what happened did not accomplish the desired outcome. Finally, in the case of program failure, the recreation program itself does not cause the appropriate action, which would have led to the accomplish-

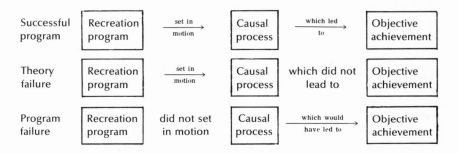

FIGURE 6.1 Types of Program Failure
SOURCE: Carol H. Weiss, *Evaluation Research*, Copyright© 1972. Reprinted by permission of Prentice-Hall, Englewood Cliffs, New Jersey.

ment of the desired outcome. It is extremely important in evaluation research to determine whether or not a recreation program is successful. However, if the program is not successful, it is equally important to determine why it failed. The researcher must remember that program evaluation seeks not to prove or disprove but to ultimately *improve* recreation and park programs. Once the type of information needed is determined, the next step in evaluation research is to select the sources of data and to choose a data collecting technique(s).

SOURCES OF RECREATION AND PARK DATA

One potential mistake researchers can make in evaluating recreation and park programs is to assume that all the data to be collected must be first-hand. In fact, careful examination of previously collected data can often extend the scope of the study, as well as save valuable time and effort. For example, the federal government periodically gathers census data on every city, county, state, and province. This data provides information and statistics on such variables as:

density of population	occupation type
size of population	per-capita income
population distribution	family income
age distribution	housing type
sex distribution	housing age
racial composition	employment rate
ethnic composition	birth rate
number of foreign born	expenditure patterns
education level	crime rate and type

Other socioeconomic, geopolitical, governmental, and community data can be obtained from such sources as:

city maps and photographs	public utility records
school records	chamber of commerce data
church records	health and welfare records
law enforcement agencies	newspaper records
real estate records	tax assessments
building permits	scouting groups
libraries	community agencies
state and federal agencies	business and professional groups
radio and TV stations	financial institutions
local colleges and universities	planning agencies

The National Recreation and Park Association annually publishes statistics and data relating to local recreation and park agencies. This information can provide comparative data on such factors as operating and capital expenditures, amount of recreation acreage, number of full- and part-time staff, population served, and a number of other recreation-related facts. In addition, town, city, and county associations often gather pertinent information that can be utilized for evaluative purposes. Two of the best local sources of information are the city planning department and the council of social agencies. Original data in the social sciences in a wide variety of areas can be obtained from a number of existing data banks and literature retrieval centers. Nasatir lists the subject matter and type of data collected for many of these libraries.[12]

Finally, the researcher should not overlook the data gathered by others in recreation or related fields. The recreation and park department and the local libraries are excellent source areas for previously conducted studies. Since recreation program usage is often dependent upon accessibility and availability, local planning departments can furnish a wealth of cogent and valuable information.

Like other forms of research, the most difficult part of the evaluation study lies in making decisions. Once the decisions have been made with respect to procedures, the work can be relatively simple. This is especially true in making data decisions. Data collection is usually not a complex undertaking, providing that proper decisions have been made before data collection begins.

DATA-GATHERING TECHNIQUES

Data can be gathered from a number of different sources and be collected by an equally large number of research instruments. Although the only limits to research techniques are the inventiveness and imagination of the researcher, Isaac and Michael offer nine functional research categories and their purposes (see Table 6.1).[13]

Examples of historical research in recreation and parks include studying racial discrimination in recreation programs over the past 50 years in the United States, tracing the history of the playground movement in Canada since the Industrial Revolution, or testing the hypothesis that Calvert Vaux was the real architect of New York's Central Park.

Examples of descriptive research include determining the status of females in public recreation programs,[14] surveying the amount of recreation and park acreage in cities, or interviewing recreation program participants in order to determine their attitudes toward the program and its staff.

TABLE 6.1   Nine Basic Methods of Research

METHOD	PURPOSE
Historical	To reconstruct the past objectively and accurately, often in relation to the tenability of a hypothesis.
Descriptive	To describe systematically a situation or area of interest factually and accurately.
Developmental	To investigate patterns and sequences of growth and/or changes as a function of time.
Case and Field	To study intensively the background, current status, and environmental interactions of a given social unit: an individual, group, institution, or community.
Correlational	To investigate the extent to which variations in one factor correspond with variations in one or more other factors based on correlation coefficients.
Causal-Comparative or "Ex Post Facto"	To investigate possible cause-and-effect relationships by observing some existing consequence and searching back through the data for plausible causal factors.
True Experimental	To investigate possible cause-and-effect relationships by exposing one or more experimental groups to one or more treatment conditions and comparing the results to one or more control groups not receiving the treatment (random assignment being essential).
Quasi-Experimental	To approximate the conditions of the true experiment in a setting which does not allow the control and/or manipulation of all relevant variables. The researcher must clearly understand what compromises exist in the internal and external validity of the design and proceed within these limitations.
Action	To develop new skills or new approaches and to solve problems with direct application to the classroom or other applied setting.

SOURCE: From S. Isaac and W. B. Michael, *Handbook in Research and Evaluation.* Published by EdITS. Copyright © 1971 by Robert R. Knapp, all rights reserved.

Examples of developmental studies include longitudinally investigating senior citizens based on an initial sample of 50 who regularly participate in recreation programs, projecting the estimated growth and need for recreation facilities in a community, or determining changing patterns of recreation participation by a cross section of children at five different age levels.

Examples of case and field studies include the case history of a mentally retarded child who loves physical recreation activities but who has a severe learning disability, an in-depth study of a group of delinquent school-age children, or a community study of how socio-economic resident characteristics relate to participation patterns in public recreation programs.

Correlation studies, for example, include an investigation of the relationships between type of recreation activity chosen and educational level of participant, a factor-analysis study of routine maintenance checklists, or a study to predict success in the recreation profession based upon correlation patterns between college grades and other educational variables.

Examples of causal-comparative studies include identification of factors related to attendance in a community recreation center using figures from data collected over the past five years, a study of the similarities and differences between those children playing inside a playground and those playing directly outside, families that camp and those who do not, or members and nonmembers of fine-art museums.

The true experimental study might include an investigation of the effects of a specific recreation activity on the behavior of emotionally disturbed boys, using random assignment to groups receiving the activity, and a control group who does not; or an investigation of the effectiveness of different methods of teaching adults to ski, using random assignments of skiers and instructurs to groups and methods.

Quasi-experimental studies in contrast to the above could use the same examples for emotionally disturbed boys or adult skiers, but subjects or methods of random assignment would not take place. When total rather than partial control of variables cannot be accomplished, then the research study becomes quasi-experimental.

The last type of research, the action study might include an examination of in-service training programs for playground leaders, the development of more meaningful techniques for leisure counseling, or an experiment with new approaches to teaching nature study to sightless children.

EXPERIMENTAL VERSUS NONEXPERIMENTAL RESEARCH

Scientific studies can be narrowed to two major categories—experimental and nonexperimental—and one or both can be used in evaluation research. Researchers tend to favor one method over the other. Physical science researchers follow the experimental design while social science researchers prefer the nonexperimental.

Experimental Research

In conducting controlled experiments, two subsamples are randomly selected from the same population, and selected characteristics of both groups are measured. One group is exposed to the program being evaluated, and a remeasurement of the selected characteristics of both groups is done. The effect of being exposed to the program is determined by comparing the extent of change between those who have been exposed (experimental group), and those who have not been exposed to the program (control group). In other words, experimental studies require that the researcher match two or more groups, administer different sets of conditions to one of them, then compare the results of the different treatments on the matched subjects.

Nonexperimental Research

Nonexperimental study does not require matching or comparisons, but rather is primarily concerned with gathering factual data. Nonexperimental study attempts to determine existing conditions rather than attempts to change any of those conditions—in other words, to determine what is, not what could be. Interviews, case studies, questionnaires, and comparison studies are examples of nonexperimental research. Which type of design should the recreation evaluator utilize?

Most recreation and parks research is nonexperimental, whereas psychological and educational research tends to be experimental. Ideally, evaluation research in recreation and parks should test hypotheses both experimentally and nonexperimentally. However, when an independent variable[15] can be controlled or manipulated, the experimental approach is the most desirable. Many important variables cannot be controlled or manipulated in social action programs. For example, skill development, aptitudes, integrity, characteristics of recreation leaders, juvenile delinquency, and home environment are specific variables, only some of which may be controlled. Ultimately, in selecting the design of an evaluation study the main criteria is: Does the design answer the research questions, and does the design adequately test the hypotheses?

There are many approaches to recreation program evaluation, but the preferred approach provides decision makers with information that is valid, reliable, and applicable. In the final analysis, the research design, model, or technique must be appropriate and specific to the program undergoing evaluation. Information produced from evaluation studies must reflect the needs of the administrators and other program personnel, and enlarge the concrete information base of ongoing programs.

SUMMARY

The task of specifying program objectives in recreation and parks is essential. Objectives are critical to program operation for without them, there can be no sound basis for the selection and implementation of activities. In addition, without objectives, there is no way in which to assess whether or not the program is successful. Program objectives must be written so as to be clear, specific, and measurable.

The first step in evaluating leisure-service programs is the conceptualization and measurement of the program's objectives. What is the program under study expected to accomplish? This initial question and the answer to it may be the most difficult part of the evaluation study. Conceptualization must be brought to bear not only on the objectives of the program itself, but also on the evaluation or measurement of these objectives. This process involves the examination of the assumptions underlying the objectives, specifying the program activities selected for their achievement, and determining *why* these activities can achieve the desired objectives.

Recreation and park evaluative data can come from a number of sources, and can be collected by an equally large number of instruments or techniques. Ultimately, the research technique selected for the evaluation study should provide the most valid, reliable, and applicable information to decision makers.

REFERENCES

¹ Tony Tripodi, Phillip Fellin, and Irwin Epstein, *Social Program Evaluation: Guidelines for Health, Education and Welfare Administrators* (Itasca, Ill.: F. E. Peacock Publishers, 1971), pp. 45–50.

² Cost-effectiveness, unlike cost-benefit approaches to program evaluation are of relatively recent origin. For an excellent analysis of this approach see John Leslie Livingstone and Sanford C. Gunn, eds., *Accounting for Social Goals: Budgeting and Analysis of Non-market Projects.* (New York: Harper & Row, 1974).

[3] Sidney G. Lutzin and Edward H. Storey, *Managing Municipal Leisure Services* (Washington, D.C.: The International City Management Association, 1973), p. 7.

[4] Richard G. Kraus and Barbara Bates, *Recreation Leadership and Supervision: Guidelines for Professional Development* (Philadelphia: W. B. Saunders Co., 1975), p. 255.

[5] Robert Mager, *Preparing Instructional Objectives* (Palo Alto, Cal: Fearon Publishers, 1975), p. 11.

[6] Norman E. Gronlund, *Stating Behavioral Objectives for Classroom Instruction* (New York: MacMillan Co., 1970), pp. 53–55.

[7] David R. Kranthwohl, Benjamin S. Bloom, and Bertram B. Masia, *Taxonomy of Educational Objectives, Handbook II: Affective Domain* (New York, David McKay Co., 1964), pp. 6–7.

[8] Mager, *Preparing Instructional Objectives*, p. 12.

[9] M. B. Unekl, A. W. Smith, and C. S. Van Doren, "Putting Computers to Good Use," *Parks and Recreation* **10**:11 (November 1975):20.

[10] Edward A. Suchman, "Evaluating Educational Programs: A Symposium," *Urban Review* 3:4 (1969):16.

[11] Carol H. Weiss, *Evaluation Research: Methods of Assessing Program Effectiveness* (Englewood Cliffs, N.J.: Prentice-Hall, 1972), p. 38.

[12] D. Nasatir, "Social Science Data Libraries," *American Sociologist* **2** (1967):207–12.

[13] Stephen Isaac and William B. Michael, *Handbook in Research and Evaluation* (San Diego: Robert R. Knapp Publishers, 1971), p. 14.

[14] William F. Theoblad, *The Female in Public Recreation: A Study of Participation and Administrative Attitudes* (Vanier City, Ontario: Canadian Park and Recreation Association, 1976), 150 pp.

[15] An independent variable is the presumed cause of the dependent variable, which is the presumed effect. The independent variable is the antecedent, while the dependent variable is the consequence.

7

MEASUREMENT IN EVALUATION RESEARCH

After the specific recreation and park program objectives have been selected for study, the next step is for the evaluator to determine the specific measures that are available and appropriate to assess the extent of objective attainment. This phase of the evaluation process is often not only the most difficult, but also the most demanding. Previous studies may have been done on similar program objectives or similar activities in related fields. If this is the case, the evaluator can save time and effort by using or modifying these measures. It may be beneficial for the evaluator to seek existing valid and reliable measures rather than attempt to develop new ones. Existing measures can be used as comparative data to help the evaluator determine whether or not the characteristics of the sample population are compatible with those being measured. For example, if the local public library or museum conducts an investigation to determine the usage characteristics of members, the information on file and the data-gathering measures may provide pertinent information to the recreation evaluator who may wish to evaluate the leisure behavior of municipal recreation program participants, a similar sample group. The library or museum data could provide information on reading habits of the same population, choice of reading material, time spent reading, attendance at museum exhibition openings, stylistic preferences of members, and other related information.

The evaluator's principal task is selecting and utilizing a technique, or combining techniques to produce the necessary information at a minimal cost.

CHOOSING THE APPROPRIATE
MEASUREMENT TOOLS

A number of evaluation techniques have successfully measured the effectiveness of program objectives. Each technique can be used at different stages of the study depending upon the evaluation objective, and can provide specific information relating to program efforts (inputs), effectiveness (outputs), and efficiency (cost-benefit).[1] These techniques are generally grouped into three general categories: monitoring techniques, empirical research techniques, and cost-analytic techniques.

Program Monitoring Techniques

Monitoring techniques include procedures used for direct program operations' review such as auditing for accountability, auditing for administrative purposes, and time-motion studies. Monitoring techniques provide a feedback mechanism to administrators: information is furnished while the program is in operation.

Program Auditing.   Auditing techniques for accountability purposes are used to review existing agency records such as program expenditures, resource allocations including staff, budget, equipment, facilities, and other operating functions. Audits are essentially reviews of existing accounting records kept by individual departments, a central institution, or municipality. As a result of law, policy, or procedure, periodic audits are conducted within operating agencies in attempts to verify the accuracy of financial statements. Typically, in both municipalities and institutions, an accounting firm is retained to review accounting procedures and certify that the recorded statement of income and expenditures is correct.

Program Accounting.   Another accounting procedure is social or client accounting. This system records information related to participants, and provides statistics on how many people were served by the program, how many participated in certain activities, how far participants traveled, and other data that could be helpful to decision makers and planners. In large metropolitan departments, this accounting function may be assigned to a research unit or other analysis section, while in smaller departments, it may be added to the responsibilities of the director or a staff member. In the case of social accounting, the system involves an appraisal of the accuracy, reliability, and existence of program records that involve program participants. The obvious benefit of social accounting is that it provides additional social information for program planners, developers, and appraisers.

Auditing for administrative purposes attempts to describe what the agency is doing in relation to existing norms or standards. More specifically, it refers to those operational methods, policies, and practices that have been established within a department, and compares them with the degree to which the department complies with them. For example, if a department has written personnel policies, the auditor attempts to determine if those policies are being followed. If they are not, the auditor will make recommendations to enable compliance or suggest policy modifications. Information from administrative audits usually concerns administrative organization or staffing patterns which may point out inconsistencies in departmental regulations and operational practices. In addition, administrative audits can provide comparative information on departmental programs such as individual activities maintenance practices and other operating features.

Program Input. The last monitoring technique, the time-and-motion study, refers to those techniques which attempt to quantify the time spent by program staff on activities under development and operation. Time-and-motion studies measure program input—that is, the amount of staff effort measured against the time devoted to a particular activity or program. One of the main functions of the time-and-motion study is to review staff resources. By determining the amount of working hours necessary for each activity in the recreation and park program, unanticipated time spent can be measured, and staff resources can be reallocated depending upon which activities are assigned a higher priority by administrators. Measurement is usually determined by the utilization of staff self-reports, determined over a prescribed time period. Daily or weekly time budgets could be initiated to measure how long each staff member spends on given activities. For example, if the time spent on programming a special event such as an easter egg hunt is out of proportion with other ongoing daily activities, a decision to drop or scale down that special event may be made. Conversely, if another special event such as community day becomes more important in the operation of the department, administrators may decide to place more staff effort on that event. Such decisions can best be made after careful consideration of departmental priorities and equally careful measurement of staff allocation.

Empirical Research Techniques

The second general technique in program evaluation are empirical research studies. These investigative methods refer to experimental, descriptive, and case-study techniques that attempt to develop, modify, and expand the body of knowledge relating to the recreation and park program. These systematic investigations, based on the scientific method, should be conducted by skilled researchers, knowledgeable in the field of recreation and parks and in the techniques of scientific investigation.

Experimental Studies. The experimental method was discussed in Chapter 6, where it was suggested that its purpose was to provide evidence that program inputs or efforts were causally related to program objective attainment. Accomplished by isolating and defining the problem and study purpose, experimental evaluation leads directly to the proposal of a treatment or program. A sample population is selected from which a representative number are randomly drawn and randomly assigned to one of two groups: experimental or control. The first group receives the program or treatment, then the two groups are compared based upon a measurement made of each group, not only before but also after the intervention of program or treatment. Examples of the experimental technique in recreation and park programs might include a study of two different methods of teaching ballroom dancing, assessing staff motivation using management by objectives, or comparing the effects of different maintenance procedures in community parks.

Descriptive Studies. A second empirical research technique is the descriptive or survey method which employs such evaluative instruments as questionnaires, interviews, participant observation, or other mainly descriptive data-collection techniques. These methods provide an accurate description of such variables as participant characteristics, public expenditures for recreation programs, or the number of participants who select one particular type of activity. Descriptive techniques can measure attendance, attitudes, opinions, income, educational level, and a number of other program variables. Descriptive research can be used at all stages of program development: initially to determine the need or interest in a certain activity, secondly to measure the extent of community participation in the planning process, and thirdly to determine the effectiveness of a designated program activity. Descriptive studies are no longer appropriate only to small populations since large-scale studies have already been conducted in geographic areas that include substantial population centers. An example of such an investigation is the Ontario Recreation Study in Canada[2] which interviewed over 10,000 individuals, 12 years of age and over in order to determine the demand for recreation by one segment of Ontario residents. Data were collected on age, sex, income, education, and geographic location of participants in 73 selected recreation activities.

Case-Studies. The case-study technique attempts to provide a detailed description of an individual, group, agency, institution, or other variable in order to comprehensively describe and explain the components of an entity. In the case of a community study, the researcher seeks to collect and examine as much data as possible regarding the community—for example, the community's history, its religious, po-litical, economic, geographical, social, and ethnic characteristics, and other related data that will provide a comprehensive picture of what makes the community under study unique. From the data the re-searcher will determine the logical interrelations of the community's various parts. This research approach differs from others in that the case-study method is directed at understanding a single case. Other research methods attempt to limit the number of variables considered, but the case-study method seeks to maximize them. For example, a given case study in recreation and parks might include a detailed examination of a midwestern community which successfully passed a controversial bond issue for purchasing additional amounts of open space for future park development. Another case study could inves-tigate the leisure behavior of an unemployed, asocial youth. In eval-uation, case-study data are particularly useful to assess program efforts in terms of staff activities, and the extent to which their activity is directly related to the achievement of program objectives.

Cost-Analysis Techniques

The third and final technique in program evaluation for recreation and parks is cost or economic analysis. As seen in Figure 7.1, these tech-niques essentially measure the benefits of program budgeting and other input-output studies that attempt to determine whether or not the program can be justified in terms of its cost on a unit or group basis. Fixed program costs in recreation include staff, facilities, equip-ment, and maintenance. The costs of each activity are determined, then the benefits (objectives if achieved) are likewise determined, and a ratio is established between the two. If the ratio is too high, an attempt is made to reduce it, presumably without affecting quality. If this cannot be done, the program is often discontinued.

Operations Research. A new type of cost-analytic technique called operations research has been used for a number of years in the military and in industry. Also called systems analysis, it utilizes mathematical and other scientific techniques that produce program models in order to make high probability predictions that certain actions will occur, providing certain recommendations are followed. Operations research attempts to develop interaction models—based upon the process of planning, demonstration, operation, and the evaluation of programs—to provide general guidelines for making the most effective use of available resources to accomplish specific objectives. Systems analysis is a highly technical method that draws heavily on mathematics and computer technology to accomplish its ends. The technical nature of

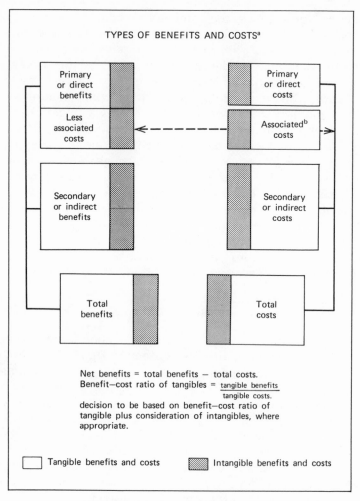

TYPES OF BENEFITS AND COSTS[a]

Net benefits = total benefits − total costs.

Benefit−cost ratio of tangibles = $\dfrac{\text{tangible benefits}}{\text{tangible costs}}$.

decision to be based on benefit−cost ratio of tangible plus consideration of intangibles, where appropriate.

☐ Tangible benefits and costs   ▨ Intangible benefits and costs

FIGURE 7.1   Benefit-Cost Analysis[3]

[a] The sizes of the boxes bear no relationship to the relative sizes of the benefits or costs.

[b] Associated costs may either be added to costs or subtracted from primary benefits.

SOURCE: W. R. D. Sewell, John David, A. D. Scott, and D. W. Ross, *Guide to Benefit-Cost Analysis* (Ottawa: Information Canada, 1965). Reproduced by permission of the Ministry of Supply and Services, Canada.

this research makes it more applicable to physical management problems than to human social problems. Churchman, et al. have provided a definitive treatment of this technique.[4] However, because of the cost and expertise required to implement this research technique, it has not found a great deal of use in the social sciences. Nevertheless, operations research and evaluation offer promise.

SECONDARY ANALYSIS

Secondary analysis consists of the examination of existing records and documents that were used but not collected by the evaluator. A secondary source can be anything written, taped, recorded, or filmed. Recreation researchers often use governmental records—such as census data, master plans, or vital statistics—as secondary sources. Other secondary sources are newspapers, magazines, books, radio and television transmissions, voting records, diaries, and letters.

Analysis of secondary materials often proves extremely fruitful since the data can cover a wide range of topics over a long period of time. For example, the Leisure Studies Data Bank at the University of Waterloo in Canada[5] has been collecting data on the leisure behavior of North Americans for a number of years. This data which include travel and vacation patterns, recreation preference studies, leisure-related personal expenditures, and other recreation information are stored on computer tapes and discs, thereby making it immediately available to students and researchers. By cross-tabulating the data, relationships among such variables as age, sex, income, family status, and education level can be determined. If a researcher wishes to determine preference for certain types of recreation activity, the computer can furnish a data printout. It is also possible to isolate one activity such as recreational boating and determine the social and economic characteristics of those respondents who regularly participate in this activity. Recreation program evaluators should not overlook the potential sources of information that secondary data can furnish.

Carter and Wharf have summarized (Tables 7.1, and 7.2, 7.3) the common uses and purposes of the three techniques of evaluation research: monitoring techniques, social research techniques, and cost-analytic techniques.[6]

MEASUREMENT VARIABLES

Ideally, evaluation research attempts to demonstrate a causal relationship between a recreation program and some desired outcome. It attempts to show that the program causes the outcome in some way, and that the outcome depends upon the program in some way. In evaluation research, both the program and the outcome are variables. However, neither the program nor the outcome are always predictable since they can vary by type or degree. Within recreation programs, not every participant has the same experience. Some participants attend an oil painting instructional program regularly, others come in-

TABLE 7.1 Monitoring Techniques

TECHNIQUE	METHOD	PURPOSE	TYPE
1. Accountability audit	• to review consistency, dependability, and accuracy of records regarding program expenditures, allocations of resources, and processing of program beneficiaries	• to establish program accountability	1. General accounting 2. Social accounting
2. Administrative audit	• to evaluate the suitability of program policies and practices • to evaluate adherence of staff practices to designated divisions of responsibility and function • to evaluate organizational patterns of work	• to provide data for planning to improve effectiveness and efficiency in administrative practices	1. Simple or focused 2. Complex or comprehensive
3. Time-Motion	• to specify the amounts of time devoted by staff to program activities • to locate uses of staff time which were not anticipated • to recommend reallocations of staff time to those activities which might be more directly related to the potential achievement of program goals	• to provide data for planning to improve effectiveness and efficiency of staff use	1. Observation 2. Self-reports 3. Sample time-and-motion study using samples of both staff and time

SOURCE: Reprinted with permission of Canadian Council on Social Development, 55 Parkdale, Ottawa, Ontario.

TABLE 7.2 Social Research Techniques

TECHNIQUE	METHOD	PURPOSE	TYPE
1. Experiments	• classical experimental design • quasi-experiments or approximations to experiments	• to provide evidence on whether or not program efforts are related causally to the accomplishment or program goals	• numerous
2. Surveys	• setting of survey objectives • designation of a target population • selection of a representative sample from that population • collection of data • accuracy checks • analysis	• descriptive function to obtain accurate facts and statements of opinion representative of the target population • explanatory function to derive possible causal connections	• flexible
3. Case	• accumulation of as much information as possible • development and use of conceptual scheme for generating ideas	• to provide detailed description of social programs as they develop for evaluation of program efforts • particularly useful for developing programs where there is difficulty in specifying objectives and in selecting programmatic means to accomplish these objectives • to pinpoint potential problems in program operation	• participant observation • informal interviews • methods of group analysis • content analysis of written documents, and so on

SOURCE: Reprinted with permission of Canadian Council on Social Development, 55 Parkdale, Ottawa, Ontario.

TABLE 7.3 Cost-Analytic Techniques

TECHNIQUE	METHOD	PURPOSE	TYPE
1. Cost accounting	• production of unit cost figures as a basis for analyzing, budgeting, and allocating resources	• to relate program costs to program outputs • to improve program budgeting • to provide information for determining program services priorities as a function of cost	(1) Cost accounting (2) Program budgeting
2. Cost-benefit analysis	• program inputs are related to program outputs or staff actions; program outputs are then related to the results of those actions • translation of criteria of goal achievement into monetary units	• to evaluate the relative effectiveness of alternative programs, strategies, and so on in terms of cost • to ascertain the relationship of costs to benefits (specified goals)	
3. Cost-outcome analysis	• to relate program costs to the results of program activities	• to gauge the relative efficiency of the costs of alternative program inputs for the accomplishment of specified objectives	
4. Operations research	• combines scientific experimentation, mathematics, statistics, and computer technology • deliberate	• to provide data on alternative ways of conducting and coordinating program activities within an organization	

SOURCE: Reprinted with permission of Canadian Council on Social Development, 55 Parkdale, Ottawa, Ontario.

termittently, while others drop out completely. Some receive greater attention from the instructor while others receive less. Some participants may be more highly motivated within the activity than others. The differences in program may result from dissimilar participants, instructor, equipment or facilities.

Program variations are important to the evaluator because they describe more fully the details of the activity and help point out why the activity is successful, or why it is not. It allows the evaluator to analyze the effects of program components to determine which parts produce better effects. For example, if a group of about-to-be retired employees participate in a pre-retirement counseling program and use their leisure time more constructively than another group who has not had such a program, the evaluator can determine the effectiveness of the counseling technique and get some indication why the program is working. If, however, only some of the participants in the program use their leisure time constructively, we can gain other insight into the process of behavioral change. Analysis of program variables can help determine why the program has the outcome it has. Once the evaluator determines which program variable has a greater effect on the outcome, he or she can recommend changes to maximize realization of program objectives.

Input Variables

There are a number of effort or input variables that every recreation and park agency adds to the program process. These variables include the stated purpose of the agency, its principles of operation, methods and techniques of planning, staffing patterns, number of people to be served, program expenditures, type of equipment, and number, type, and location of facility resources. Just as the agency adds input variables to the recreation program, so, too, do participants. There are a number of different characteristics of participants that add to program variations, including age, sex, income, occupation, education, race, and other socioeconomic factors. In addition, participants bring to recreation programs different attitudes and opinions about the activity, expectations from the program, motivations for participation and previous experience in recreation activity. The evaluator must realize that the program can affect some participant characteristics and program variables, but not others. Therefore, it is important to collect data on both participant and program variables since both types of information help define whether or not a program is successful, and why this is so.

Intervening Variables

A second type of variable in recreation and park programs is the intervening variable—a condition or circumstance that exists between the program and its outcome that may directly or indirectly affect the program outcome. In the normal program sequence, the activity is planned, resources are allocated, the activity is begun, and finally it is evaluated. The program inputs are planning and resource allocation, and output becomes objective achievement measured through evaluation. However, an intervening variable might influence the outcome of the evaluation. For instance, a park landscaping program is planned to reseed a grassy highway divider. Based upon previous experience, if adequate resources are allocated to the project, then new growth should occur. However, if there is insufficient rainfall (which might not be normal), the expected result of new growth might not occur. Also, if an important art museum were planning a major loan exhibition of paintings by Joan Miro, and immediately prior to the museum's mounting the exhibition, one of the major contributors suddenly died and the estate would not adhere to the terms of the agreement, this intervening variable might well force cancellation, or at least alter the scope of the exhibition.

Intervening variables in a recreation program may occur spontaneously (such as inclement weather or instructor illness), or they may be manipulated by program personnel (adding an extra week to an existing instructional program). In either event, these variables often affect the program's outcome. If intervening variables cannot be controlled, the evaluator must be aware of their existence, and analyze them as any other variable. Just as it is important to determine what effect the program had in reaching its objective, so too is it important to determine whether the program's outcomes were affected by intervening variables.

RELIABILITY AND VALIDITY

There is no one, single decision or technique suitable for every recreation and park program evaluation. The selection of appropriate procedures depends upon the question(s) to be answered, the purpose of the evaluator, and the intended use of the evaluation study. However, the design or technique selected for the evaluation must be both valid and reliable. Validity refers to the degree to which the measurement procedure succeeds in fulfilling what it was intended to do. Reliability refers to the degree to which the measurement procedure can obtain consistent results upon repeated application. While a great deal has been written about these two concepts, there is still a great deal of misunderstanding in relation to evaluation research.

Objectivity

Ensuring objectivity is not simply a matter of determining the right organizational structure for evaluation. It is also a matter of paying careful attention to the design and selection of instruments for the evaluation study. When utilizing a questionnaire or interview guide, questions must not be suggestive. In addition, the questionnaire must be so structured or the interviews conducted that respondents are not influenced to respond in a specific pattern.

Reliability and validity are interdependent: there can be no validity without reliability. However, there can be a high degree of reliability without validity. Since a given data-gathering technique must be reliable if it is to be valid, variables that tend to lower reliability may also cause low validity. On the other hand, variables or factors that cause low validity may not even affect the reliability of an instrument. For example, a person can be tested for content recall—how many random characters or events in a story-telling program can be repeated—very reliably, but these test scores would be quite invalid as a measure of creativity.

A fundamental criteria of sound evaluation design is validation of the study—that is, determining the extent to which evaluation information obtained is accurate and truthful. There are a number of difficulties inherent in attaining complete validity, such as the repression of facts people would rather forget, the frailty of human memory, the tendency to exaggerate enjoyable events, and the extent to which respondents will give the information they feel is expected. The well-designed evaluation research study will establish a series of cross-checks to enable the evaluator to judge the validity of the data.

It has been suggested that reliability is the extent to which an evaluation instrument will consistently produce the same result, with the same respondents. Again, it is difficult to retain absolute reliability. Individuals may feel differently from day to day, and so may well respond differently to the same question that is asked at different times. In addition, respondents may answer differently depending upon the situation in which they are asked the question. Good evaluation research design will attempt to ensure that these potential variations are taken into account, cross-checked where possible, and limited to those variables over which the evaluator has no control. The research design must be standardized so no one interviewer or researcher's behavior will influence the respondents' answers. Therefore, in conducting an evaluation study, the researcher must not only select a technique that affords the greatest possible degree of objectivity, validity, and reliability, but must also select one that is sufficiently flexible to provide maximum communication with respondents.

MEASURING PROGRAM EFFECTS

In evaluating recreation and park programs, the process must be analyzed in terms of the characteristics of the program, participants involved in the program, the location in which the program takes place, and the effects produced by the program. Each of these four elements must be specified and analyzed in order to determine an answer to specific questions raised in program evaluation.

The attributes of the recreation program that make it successful or unsuccessful must also be specified, and must attempt to identify and diagnose specific causes of program success or failure. Specification of program characteristics requires an analysis of the program's component parts and the identification of those aspects which detract from or contribute to program effectiveness. For example, inadequate provision for safety might negate an otherwise successful swimming program. Conversely, a new kiln or wheel might make a pottery program more successful.

The participants involved in the recreation program should also be specified. What age group are most affected by the program? Who does the program succeed in reaching and who does it not reach? What is the best population for the program: the individual, the group, the general public? Does selection of participants influence the outcome of the program? Do participants influence others enrolled in the program?

The situation or conditions in which the program operates must be specified to determine whether or not they contribute to program success or failure. The physical location, program sponsorship, timing, and other conditions may influence the program outcome. For instance, if a dramatic program were set up outdoors instead of inside a community center, would it be as successful, less successful, or more successful? Does it depend upon the production—Wilder's *Our Town* or Miller's *Death of a Salesman*? If a hockey league were sponsored by a voluntary agency instead of a municipal recreation and park department, would it be as successful?

Finally, the most important specification which must be made is to identify the effects produced by the program. Which aspects of the final program outcomes should be used as judgment criteria? Obviously, effects can be anticipated on the basis of individuals enrolled in the program, the program itself, the organization sponsoring the program, and the leaders directly involved in the program operation.

Obviously, the number and extent to which these characteristics or specifications are included in an evaluation study will largely depend upon the program objectives, the administrative support given to the study, and the amount of available research resources. Sound research design when combined with evaluative data contributes to basic knowledge as well as administrative decision making in recreation and parks.

EFFECTS OF EVALUATION

In large measure, techniques that measure program effectiveness depend on the objectives of the program. Data-collection instruments in recreation program evaluation may attempt to measure such variables as:

1. Attitudes and opinions of participants.
2. Values held in relation to personal leisure.
3. Age, sex, disability type, and other participant characteristics.
4. Knowledge of participants toward recreation activity.
5. Leisure behavior before, during or after activity.

Other variables that program evaluation may wish to measure could concern not only participants, but the activity or program, the leaders, the agency sponsoring the activity, and other individuals or groups whom the program influences.

Measures of Change

In recreation programs for special populations,[7] the majority of evaluation studies tend to be individual in nature and attempt to assess changes (physical or psychological) in program participants. These evaluations may utilize techniques to assess disabilities, attitudes, personality traits, and other behavioral characteristics. Each variable may be directly related to program objectives. For example, a handicraft program may expect to impart basic knowledge about the activity, specific skills (such as eye-hand coordination), and certain values and attitudes toward recreation activity. Many such programs attempt to modify or change behavior as well. Rather than interviews, questionnaires, or tests, other sources of data may be necessary to assess behavioral change. Information relating to client or participant behavior can be collected from individual self-reports or by reports by people who have contact with the client. In many therapeutic institutions, data are obtained on individuals from a group meeting of staff members who assess the progress of each client. In hospitals this treatment team may consist of the doctor, nurse, social worker, and physical, occupational, and recreation therapist, or others directly involved in the treatment process. Client observation is another source of data used in some evaluation studies.

Measures of Attitude

In all recreation programs, therapeutic or municipal, the majority of evaluations tend to rely heavily on more easily obtained attitudinal measures. However, the overwhelming proportion of recreation programs are, or should be concerned with behavioral change as the result of recreation activity. An example of behavioral change in terms of a hypothetical question for measurement might be: Does participation in an institutional recreation program for the aged lead to a decrease in social isolation, which in turn leads to a more meaningful life? Or: Does participation in a social recreation program for delinquent youth lead to a change in attitude toward society, which in turn leads to a less asocial life? Behavioral change is difficult to measure, especially in municipal recreation programs where many administrators do not know specifically what they expect their programs to accomplish. Behavioral measures are not always available, and even where they do exist, they may not be appropriate to measure changes in leisure behavior. For example, how should one measure and quantify an increase in neurotic behavior? The measurement problems are incomprehensible.

Measures of Opinion

One of the most widely used measures of recreation program effectiveness are opinions of participants toward the program. They are asked: did they enjoy it, what did they like most about it, like least about it, whether they would participate in another, if they would recommend it to a friend, how could it be improved, and other similar questions. Obviously, there is some justification in determining whether or not the program had participant appeal, but it is equally obvious that if it were a total failure, no one would come. However, people often participate in recreation programs for different reasons, and often these reasons are totally unrelated to the program objectives. Some people may participate in a community tennis program for the exercise it gives them, others because they are want to improve their skill levels, while others see tennis as a status activity and participate in it in order to be seen by others they wish to emulate. Since the majority of public recreation administrators never propose specific objectives for their programs, there is no way participants can meaningfully assess its effectiveness. Therefore, participant opinions are solely an indication of their individual interests, and responses are generally irrelevant to the purpose of the program. Recreation programs—whether in communities, institutions, or at national congresses—that are based on the "popularity contest" approach to evaluation are woefully inadequate indicators of program effectiveness. Donald Campbell suggests that this evaluation approach can also be called "Grateful Testimonials":

> *Human courtesy and gratitude being what it is, the most dependable means of assuring a favorable evaluation is to use voluntary testimonials for those who have had the treatment (program). If the spontaneously produced testimonials are in short supply, these should be solicited from the recipients with whom the program is still in contact. The rosy glow resulting is analogous to the professor's impression of his teaching success when it is based solely upon the comments of those students who come up and talk with him after class . . .* [8]

Some recreation and park departments commission evaluation studies to produce or suggest changes in their delivery of services. They may seek new approaches to make their programs more responsive to local citizens or to broaden their scope of services. With this type of evaluation study, the measure of program effectiveness is predicated upon agency characteristics. In-house data such as total budget, expenditures devoted to specific activities, staff deployment, and resource allocation can be extrapolated by the researcher. In recreation and park programs, the use of checklists that have been developed by experts as standards of service have long been used as evaluation techniques. Checklists and other similar techniques cannot be considered as either valid or reliable methods of determining program effectiveness, but rather should be considered as indicators of what are popularly accepted good practices. The major difficulty with these checklists are that they become law over time, and rather than being accepted as *minimum* standards of service, they become the "ideal." In addition, recreators must realize that checklists are indicators of program *input*—number of staff assigned, number of dollars allocated, type of facilities provided, and so on. They become intervening variables and not measures of program *output*. Checklist items may be useful for purposes of accreditation, for providing staff and the public with criteria for service, or for monitoring the departments' program activities. However, they cannot be measures of evaluation research since they relate to effort (what the department puts in), rather than effectiveness (what the outcome of this effort is). Sound program evaluation provides the opportunity to test whether or not these checklist items are in fact related to successful program outcomes. Figure 7.2 depicts the causal sequence of a recreation program.

The program sequence for recreation programs begins with the establishment of specific objectives and resource allocations. The causal sequence then sets in motion a series of actions or events which may bring about the desired outcome. Without intervening variables, we assume a direct causal relationship between the program (cause) and attaining the desired objective (effect). However, in the case with intervening variables between the cause and the effect, the preconditions again establish the program operation, but once the program has begun, an increase or decrease in those preconditions may directly affect program objective attainment. Again, it must be remembered in this instance that these intervening variables are measures of *input*, not measures of effectiveness since the degree to which recreation and park departments change or modify resources com-

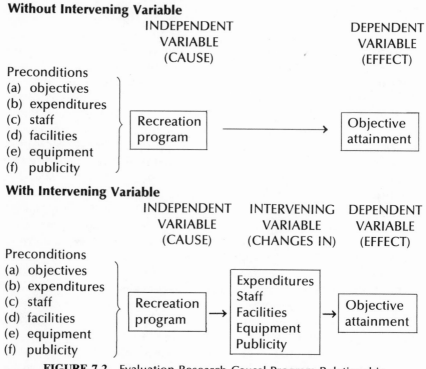

FIGURE 7.2 Evaluation Research Causal Program Relationship

mitted to programs may be in direct proportion to the degree to which the program objectives are achieved.

CONTEMPORARY EVALUATION MODELS

The literature on program evaluation indicates a number of differing views that authors hold toward some aspects of the evaluation process. Although these views are primarily directed toward education and social program assessment, nevertheless, they are extremely important to recreation and parks since they provide comparative descriptions of evaluation. Worthen and Sanders have proposed a multipage matrix (Table 7.4) which describes individual differences between these contemporary approaches and proposes to compare them by suggesting twelve important evaluation considerations.

Which model or technique should be used to evaluate recreation and park programs? Each of the eight models proposed could be used, depending upon the purpose of the evaluation study. A few might have to be modified for recreation use, but it is important to review the purpose of each model:

1. Robert Stake's model would need little modification to fit the purpose of recreation program evaluation. However, the essential element of this approach is the emphasis on a formal inquiry process, one that has had little acceptance in the field of recreation and parks.
2. Michael Scriven's model, and variations of it, have been used in recreation program evaluation, but on a far less objective basis than that he proposes.
3. Malcolm Provus relates back to the standards approach to evaluation, one that recreators will feel comfortable with. However, it is a much more sophisticated approach, one that requires considerable expenditures of staff, time, and effort.
4. The Robert Hammond model seeks to determine the extent that innovation or creativity is effective in achieving program objectives. It stresses the measurement of behavioral objectives, which the majority of recreators are unsure or unwilling to determine.
5. Daniel Stufflebeam's model is appealing to recreation administrators since it provides them with decision-making information. However, like the Stake and Scriven models, it requires a formal research inquiry.
6. Marvin Alkin's model has been used successfully to evaluate mental health programs. It emphasizes a systems approach to

TABLE 7.4 Comparisons of Contemporary

	STAKE	SCRIVEN	PROVUS	HAMMOND
Definition	Describing and judging an educational program.	Gathering and combining performance data with weighted set of goal scales.	Comparing performance against standards.	Assessing effectiveness of current and innovative programs at the local level by comparing behavioral data with objectives.
Purpose	To describe and judge educational programs based on a formal inquiry process.	To establish and justify merit or worth. Evaluation plays many roles.	To determine whether to improve, maintain, or terminate a program.	To find out whether innovation is effective in achieving expressed objectives.
Key Emphasis	Collection of descriptive and judgmental data from various audiences.	Justification of data gathering instruments, weightings, and selection of goals. Evaluation model: combining data on different performance scales into a single rating.	Identifying discrepancies between standards and performance using team approach.	Local program development.
Role of Evaluator	Specialist concerned with collecting, processing, and interpreting descriptive and judgmental data.	Responsible for judging the merit of an educational practice for producers (formative) and consumers (summative).	A team member who aids program improvement and counsels administration; also should be independent of the program unit.	Consultant who should provide expertise in data collection; should be also a trainer of local evaluators (program personnel).
Relationship to Objectives	Examination of goal specifications and priorities. Identification of areas of failures and successes. It is up to the evaluator to assist in writing behavioral objectives.	Look at goals and judge their worth. Determine whether they are being met.	Agreement of evaluation team and program staff on standards. Comparison of performance against standards to see whether a discrepancy exists.	Evaluation focuses on the definition and measurement of behavioral objectives.
Relationship to Decision Making	Descriptive and judgmental data result in reports (including recommendations) to various audiences. Judgments may be based on either absolute or relative standards.	Evaluation reports (with judgments explicitly stated for producers or consumers) used in decision making.	Evaluation staff collects information essential to program improvement and notes discrepancies between performance and standards. Every question involves a criterion (C), new information (I), and a decision (D). Evaluator provides the new information.	Evaluation is the source on which to base decisions about instructional, institutional, and behavioral dimensions.

146

Evaluation Models on Selected Characteristics

STUFFLEBEAM	ALKIN	PERSONAL JUDGMENT (e.g., Accreditation)	TYLER
Defining, obtaining, and using information for decision making.	The process of ascertaining the decision areas of concern, selecting appropriate information, and collecting and analyzing information.	Focusing attention on processes or education using professional judgment. Development of standards for educational programs.	Comparing student performance with behaviorally stated objectives.
To provide relevant information to decision makers.	To report summary data useful to decision makers in selecting among alternatives.	To identify deficiencies in the education of teachers and students relevant to content and procedures, self-improvement.	To determine the extent to which purposes of a learning activity are actually being realized.
Evaluation reports used for decision making.	Evaluation reports used for decision making.	Personal judgment used in evaluating processes of education; self-study.	Specification of objectives and measuring learning outcomes of pupils.
Specialist who provides evaluation information to decision makers.	Specialist who provides evaluation information to decision makers.	Professional colleagues who make recommendations—a professional judge.	Curriculum specialist who evaluates as part of curriculum development and assessment.
Terminal stage in context eval. is setting objectives; input eval. produces ways to reach objectives; product evaluation determines whether objectives are reached.	Range and specificity of program objectives determined in systems assessment; program planning produces ways to reach objectives, program improvement provides data on the extent to which objectives are being achieved; program certification determines whether objectives are reached.	Self-study judgments are based on sets of predetermined criteria.	Evaluation implies attainment of behavioral objectives stated at the beginning of the course.
Evaluation provides information for use in decision making.	Evaluation provides information for use in decision making.	When deficiencies are found, program revisions are requested, thus correcting substandard conditions; corrective process built in.	Actual pupil performance data will provide information for the decision maker to use on strengths and weaknesses of a course or curriculum.

TABLE 7.4 (continued)

	STAKE	SCRIVEN	PROVUS	HAMMOND
Types of Evaluation	(1) Formal vs. informal.	(1) Formative—summative. (2) Comparative—noncomparative (3) Intrinsic—payoff. (4) Mediated.	(1) Design. (2) Installation. (3) Process. (4) Product. (5) Cost.	(1) Instructional dimension. (2) Institutional dimension. (3) Behavioral dimension used for describing programs.
Constructs Proposed	(1) Data matrices: description (intents and observations) and judgment. (2) Processing descriptive data: contingency among antecedents, transactions, outcomes, congruence between intents and observations. (3) Bases for forming absolute and relative judgments.	(1) Distinction between goals (claims) and roles (functions). (2) Several types of evaluation.	(1) Discrepancy concept. (2) Feedback and revision of objectives and/or program.	(1) The application of evaluation design to existing program. (2) Decisions about adequacy of current program in relationship to the objectives. (3) Feedback from (2) leads to innovation. (4) Application of evaluation to innovation itself. (5) Notion that feedback could continue.
Criteria for Judging Evaluation	(1) Should be panoramic, not microscopic. (2) Should include descriptive and judgmental data. (3) Should provide immediate relative answers for decision making. (4) Should be formal (objective, scientific, reliable.)	(1) Should be predicated on goals. (2) Must indicate worth. (3) Should have construct validity. (4) Should be a wholistic program evaluation.	(1) Team involvement. (2) Assume one-to-one correspondence between design and solution. (3) Compare performance against standards as a tool for improvement and assessment. (4) Periodic feedback.	(1) Related to behavioral objectives. (2) An ongoing process. (3) Provides feedback on goal achievement for program modification. (4) Uses local personnel, and is part of local educational program.
Implications for Design	Very general structure. Matrices should be included in design.	(1) Look at many factors. (2) Be involved in value judgments. (3) Require use of scientific investigations. (4) Evaluate from within (formative) or from without (summative).	(1) Provide continuous evaluation (feedback loops). (2) Provide relevant and timely information for making decisions. (3) Provide cost-benefit analysis. (4) Involvement of evaluation in program development.	(1) Use of multivariate structure—focus on interactions of dimensions. (2) Generate empirical research. (3) Necessity for inclusion of local personnel.

STUFFLEBEAM	ALKIN	PERSONAL JUDGMENT (e.g., Accreditation)	TYLER
(1) Context. (2) Input. (3) Process. (4) Product.	(1) Systems assessment. (2) Program planning. (3) Program implementation. (4) Program improvement. (5) Program certification.	(1) Self-study. (2) Visitation. (3) Annual reports. (4) Evaluation panels.	Pre-post measurement of performance.
(1) Context evaluation for planning decisions. (2) Input evaluation for programming decisions (3) Process evaluation for implementing decisions. (4) Product evaluation for recycling decisions.	Evaluation of educational systems vs. evaluation of instructional programs; five areas of evaluation.	Use of content specialists as judges.	(1) Statements of objectives in behavioral terms. (2) Teaching objectives are pupil-oriented. (3) Objectives must consider: pupil's entry behavior, analysis of our culture, school philosophy, learning theories, new developments in teaching, etc.
(1) Internal validity. (2) External validity. (3) Reliability. (4) Objectivity. (5) Relevance. (6) Importance. (7) Scope. (8) Creditibility. (9) Timeliness. (10) Pervasiveness. (11) Efficiency.	Information provided to a decision maker should be effective and not confusing or misleading. Appropriate evaluation procedures should be used for different decisions.	(1) Reflects interests of program administrators. (2) Standard criteria often used.	(1) Behavioral objectives clearly stated.
(1) Experimental design not applicable. (2) Use of systems approach for evaluation studies. (3) Directed by administrator.	Evaluation domain determined by the decision maker; the objects of evaluation vary along a continuum from discrete, definable objects to complex systems.	(1) Involvement of professional community. (2) Quick feedback.	(1) Need to interpret and use results of assessment. (2) Develop designs to assess student progress.

TABLE 7.4 (continued)

	STAKE	SCRIVEN	PROVUS	HAMMOND
Contributions	(1) Provides a systematic method for arranging descriptive and judgmental data, thus emphasizing inter- and intra-relations between them. (2) Considers both absolute and relative judgment. (3) Requires explicit standards. (4) Generalizability of the model.	(1) Discriminates between formative (ongoing) and summative (end) evaluation. (2) Focus on direct assessment of worth, focus on value. (3) Applicable in diverse contexts. (4) Analysis of means and ends. (5) Delineation of types of evaluation. (6) Evaluation of objectives.	(1) Provides continuous communication between program and evaluation staff through feedback loops. (2) Allows for program improvement as well as assessment either at early stages or at end. (3) Acknowledges alternative procedures in adjusting objectives and in changing treatment. (4) Forces explicit statement of standards.	(1) Makes use of local personnel who can carry on evaluation process once initiated. (2) Considers inter-action of several dimensions and variables. (3) Provides feedback on program development and revisions: stresses self-evaluation. (4) Requires specification of behavioral objectives.
Limitations	(1) Inadequate methodology for obtaining information on key constructs. (2) Some cells of design matrix overlap, some distinctions not clear. (3) Possibility of leading to internal strife within program; value conflicts possible.	(1) Equating performance on different criteria and assigning relative weights to criteria creates methodological problems. (2) No methodology for assessing validity of judgments. (3) Several overlapping concepts.	(1) Demands a lengthy time commitment; may be expensive to carry through. (2) Inadequate methodology for establishing standards. (3) Requires large, expert, well-articulated staff. (4) Designed for complete evaluation; partial evaluation not considered.	(1) Difficulty of quantifying data involving several dimensions and variables. (2) May be complex and time-consuming to set up. (3) Possible fixation of evaluation on the "cube." (4) Neglects judgmental dimension. (5) Motivation problem in local personnel.

Basis of Comparisons:
Robert E. Stake, "The Countenance of Educational Evaluation," *Teachers College Record,* 68(1967):523–40.
Michael Scriven, "The Methodology of Evaluation," in *Perspectives of Curriculum Evaluation,* ed. R. W. Tyler (Chicago: Rand McNally, 1967), 39–83.
Malcolm Provus, "Evaluation of Ongoing Programs in the Public School Systems," *The Sixty-eighth Yearbook of the National Society for the Study of Education* (Chicago: University of Chicago Press. 1969), Part II, 242–83.
Robert L. Hammond, "Evaluation at the Local Level," EPIC Evaluation Center, Tucson, Arizona (mimeo, n.d.).
Daniel L. Stufflebeam, "Evaluation as Enlightenment for Decision-Making," Ohio State University Evaluation Center (mimeo, 1968).

STUFFLEBEAM	ALKIN	PERSONAL JUDGMENT (e.g., Accreditation)	TYLER
(1) Provides a service function by supplying data to administrators and decision makers charged with conduct of the program. (2) Is sensitive to feedback. (3) Allows for evaluation to take place at any stage of the program. (4) Wholistic.	(1) Provides a service function to administrators and decision makers. (2) Allows for evaluation to take place at any stage of the program. (3) Wholistic.	(1) Is easy to implement; team can observe and make judgment. (2) Has little lag time between observations made, data collected, and feedback. (3) Breadth of variables noted is large. (4) Leads to self-study habit and self-improvement.	(1) Is easy to assess whether behavioral objectives are being achieved. (2) Is easy for practitioners to design evaluative studies. (3) Checks degree of congruency between performance and objectives; focus on clear definition of objectives.
(1) Little emphasis on value concerns. (2) Decision-making process is unclear; methodology undefined. (3) May be costly and complex if used entirely. (4) Not all activities are clearly evaluative.	(1) Role of values in evaluation unclear. (2) Description of decision-making process incomplete. (3) May be costly and complex. (4) Not all activities are clearly evaluative.	(1) Objectivity and empirical basis are questionable. (2) Attention to process of education not balanced by attention to consequences. (3) Replicability is questionable.	(1) Tendency to oversimplify program and focus on terminal rather than ongoing and preprogram information. (2) Tendency to focus directly and narrowly on objectives, with little attention to worth of the objectives.

Marvin C. Alkin, "Evaluation Theory Development," *UCLA CSE Evaluation Comment,* No. 2(1969):2-7.

National Study of Secondary School Evaluation, *Evaluative Criteria, 1960 Edition* (Washington, D.C.: National Study of Secondary School Evaluation, 1960).

Ralph W. Tyler, "General Statement on Evaluation," *Journal of Educational Research,* 35(1942):492-501.

SOURCE: From *Educational Evaluation: Theory and Practice* by Blaine R. Worthen and James R. Sanders. Copyright © 1973 by Wadsworth Publishing Company, Inc., Belmont, Cal. 94002. Reprinted by permission of the publisher.

evaluation and offers a unique opportunity for making program decisions based upon selection of alternatives.

7. Somewhat similar to the Provus model, the personal judgment approach to evaluation relies on standards proposed by experts in the field. It is the weakest of the evaluation techniques proposed, but the one most used in recreation and parks today.

8. The final approach, Ralph Tyler's, is concerned with learning behavior. Although it relies heavily on the use of standardized tests, nevertheless it offers recreators the potential to measure in behavioral terms, the effectiveness of their instructional programs.

Whichever model or approach to recreation program evaluation is selected, it must be based upon clear, specific, and measurable objectives. Objective specification is essential to program evaluation, and if there is one point on which the authors of the eight models agree, it is that objectives are central to the evaluation study. Any evaluation requires a commitment on the part of the recreation administrator, staff, and others who are involved in the program. This commitment must be predicated on the assumption that any program, recreation or otherwise, is capable of improvement. Again, it is important to reiterate that the purpose of evaluation is not to prove or disprove, but to improve the recreation program.

THE RECREATION PROGRAM EVALUATION PROCESS

There is no standardized or uniform formula for administrators or evaluators to select the "best" design or method of pursuing an evaluation study. Selection of designs and research techniques depends upon the study's intended uses, the decisions to be made, and the information needs of the sponsoring agency. It is unfortunate that much also depends upon the limitations of the agency itself—the restrictions placed on the study by the realities of time, location, and people. An additional limitation is often the matter of funding. Too often there are no funds allocated for an evaluation study, and even when they are available, they are usually quite limited. Low-funding levels impose inevitable restrictions on how much of the program can be studied and for how long. Therefore, the choice of evaluation methods often appears to be a compromise between the ideal and the feasible.

The evaluation study process has very little difference from what has come to be expected of any well organized research design. Evaluation, like research, normally adheres to the following sequence:

1. Statement of the problem.
2. Purpose(s) of the study.
3. Basic assumptions.
4. Study hypotheses.
5. Definition of terms.
6. Limitations and delimitations of the study.
7. Review of related literature and research.
8. Methodology and procedures of the study.
9. Presentation and analysis of findings.
10. Summary, conclusions and recommendations.

However, unlike a solitary investigator who pursues the answer to a research problem, the evaluator never operates alone. In order for the study to be effective, the evaluator must become personally involved with administrators, supervisors, leaders, participants, and any others associated with the recreation program under study. Although the actual conduct of the evaluation study may follow the same sequence as other types of research, the initial stage of the evaluation process is quite different.

Rationale for Evaluation

The decision to conduct an evaluation study usually arises from a decision makers need to answer program-based questions. A second rationale for evaluation stems from the administrators' need for more information to better choose between program alternatives. This is the best stage to decide to evaluate the recreation program and to select the evaluator. At this early stage, the evaluator trys to determine the specific information needs of the administrator, and gathers together all the written information the department has with respect to its purpose, goals, and objectives. The decision to evaluate sets in motion the evaluation process (see Figure 7.3). Next to each step in the evaluation process an indication is made suggesting which individuals or groups should be involved.

Program Evaluation Model

Although it has been suggested that there is no one, single model of program evaluation that is suitable for all recreation and park applications, Figure 7.4 offers a unified paradigm of program evaluation that may be useful to practitioners.

PROCESS	ADMINISTRATOR	EVALUATOR	STAFF	PARTICIPANTS	PUBLIC
1. Expressed need for evaluation from questions or alternatives about the program.	X				
2. Determination of goals.	X	X	X	X	X
3. Establishing general objectives.	X	X	X	X	X
4. Establishing specific objectives.	X	X	X		
5. Deciding what to evaluate.	X	X			
6. Specifying evaluation objectives.	X	X	X		
7. Choosing an evaluation design.	X	X	X		
8. Determining measures of objective achievement.	X	X	X		
9. Discussion of the evaluation design.	X	X	X	X	
10. Choosing the activity or program to evaluate.	X	X	X		
11. Choosing the sample.	X	X			
12. Gathering the evaluation data.	X	X	X		
13. Analyzing the evaluation data.		X			
14. Discussion of the findings.	X	X	X		
15. Presenting the study findings.		X			
16. Discussion of recommendations.	X	X	X		
17. Presenting program recommendations.		X			
18. Implementing the recommendations.	X		X		

FIGURE 7.3 Evaluation Process and Its Participants

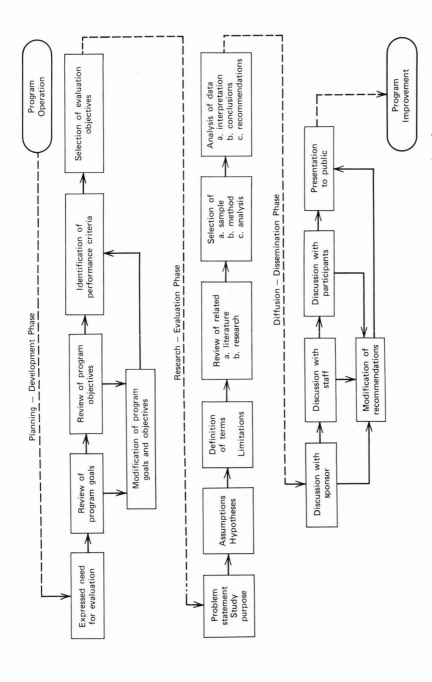

FIGURE 7.4 A Unified Model of Program Evaluation for Recreation and Parks

The planning-development phase begins with the recognition that there is a program problem, or that some decision relating to a specific program must be made, thus creating the need for an evaluation study. A review of the program goals and objectives is made with the administrator and the staff. If the goals and objectives are unclear, are interpreted differently, or are nonexistent, modifications are made or goals and objectives are then established. Specific performance criteria to measure program objective achievement are identified. The final step in the planning-development phase is the joint selection of evaluation objectives to determine specifically what is to be evaluated. The administrator and evaluator must agree on this point because once the study has been completed, and the results do not provide information that the administrator seeks, the entire study may well be an exercise in futility.

The second phase, the research-evaluation study, initially identifies both the problem involved and the purpose(s) of the investigation. Basic assumptions and/or hypotheses may be proposed although they are not crucial to every evaluation study. Unique or potentially misunderstood terms are defined, and both limitations and delimitations of the study are enumerated. Any previous studies or literature relating to the department or to similar departments are reviewed to provide current data or perspectives. A sample is then selected, either specific activities and/or participants. Data-gathering instruments and data-analysis techniques are selected. Then the evaluation study proceeds to be conducted. Finally, the results of the evaluation are analyzed and interpreted, and from this data, conclusions and recommendations are presented. With respect to program improvement, a number of alternative suggestions may be presented, but, ultimately, the evaluator must select from recommendations those which have the most utility and practicality.

The diffusion-dissemination phase of the investigation begins when the evaluator presents the findings and makes recommendations to the administrator, staff, and, if appropriate, to program participants. Based upon the results of these discussion, the evaluator may choose to make certain revisions or modifications to the final written report, which is then presented to the sponsoring department and to the general public.

An example of such a model for program evaluation may be seen from the following illustration. The manager of a large state park may have received complaints about the quality of exhibits in the park historical museum. In addition, the number of visitors during the past year has decreased at the rate of approximately 4 percent per month. None of the staff can propose a viable cause for this situation, so the manager seeks to have the museum exhibits evaluated in order to determine the cause(s).

An evaluator is selected and together with the manager and staff, he begins to review the goals and objectives of the museum program. One of the most significant findings of this process is the realization that although the museum goals are appropriate, there are no written objectives for suggesting the task to be accomplished. The evaluator and the staff agree on a set of objectives that are clear, specific, and measurable. Next, they identify guidelines or criteria to help determine how the objectives will be measured. The final task of this initial phase is to select and agree upon the objectives of the evaluation itself, or more simply, what the evaluation hopes to accomplish.

From the previous information gained during the process of the planning-development phase, the evaluator succinctly states the problem as underutilization of the museum exhibit program. The purposes of the study are (1) to determine the cause of this problem and (2) to make specific recommendations that will enhance public participation in the program. For the purposes of this study, no assumptions or hypotheses were made. After defining the terminology in the study, the evaluator decides to limit the investigation to potential users of the museum and to limit the duration of the study to a twelve-month period. All printed information about the museum, its collection, and exhibits is reviewed. In addition, any similar literature and studies that deal with the problem of underutilization of museum exhibits is also reviewed. The sample consists of a randomly selected group of visitors, both entering and exiting from the exhibits, as well as a number of individuals who have signed the guestbook and provided addresses during the past calendar year. The methodology selected consists of (1) a mail questionnaire to individuals selected from names in the guestbook, (2) a short, sequence-structured interview of those individuals who have or will see the exhibits, and (3) a duration-interval measurement to determine the amount of time visitors spend viewing individual exhibits. The analysis technique will consist of frequency distributions, percentages, and cross-tabulations with regard to age, sex, occupation, income, education, and number of previous visits to other museums (of all types). After the study has been completed, and the data both tabulated and analyzed, the evaluator proposed a series of recommendations:

1. Changing individual exhibits with greater frequency.
2. Hiring two additional curatorial staff and a Director of Education.
3. Soliciting nationally for additional exhibition material pertinent

to the museum locale and the genre of the permanent collection.

4. Adding 30 new parking spaces adjacent to the museum entrance.
5. Purchasing and installing professional exhibition panels and a rear screen projector.
6. Enlarging the scope of the museum permanent collection in order to appeal to greater visitor diversity.
7. Embarking on a major fund-raising drive or capital campaign in order to enlarge the size of the museum.
8. Installing an air-conditioning system.
9. Establishing a volunteer docent program in order to provide group visitor tours.
10. Providing in-service training program on the museum and its collection for the entire park staff.

The evaluator discusses the findings and recommendations with the administrator and the staff. Additional recommendations might arise, or recommendations might be modified or deleted depending upon practicality and the limitations of potential for use. After any revisions are made, the evaluator submits the final report to the sponsoring organization, then to the public with a suggested method and time-table for implementation. What happens to this information after the evaluator presents it is the subject of the next chapter.

SUMMARY

To ensure objectivity in evaluation research is not simply a matter of determining the appropriate organizational structure. It is also a matter of paying careful attention to all aspects of the research design.

The second fundamental of sound evaluation research is that of maximizing validity—the extent to which information obtained is both accurate and truthful. The adequately designed evaluation research study should establish a series of cross-checks so that the evaluator may judge the validity of the data obtained.

Reliability is the extent to which any particular research method will consistently produce the same result from the same people. Adequately designed evaluation research will endeavor to ensure that variations are taken into account, cross-checked where possible, and limited to those factors over which the evaluator has no control.

Although it is theoretically possible to make a clear distinction between these three concepts, they will often be closely interrelated in practice. Complete standardization of the research method which achieves the greatest possible degree of objectivity, validity, and reliability, but which at the same time allows for sufficient flexibility to provide maximum information to decision makers, is the sought-after ideal.

There are a number of measurement models and techniques available for recreation and park program evaluations. However, there is no one single method appropriate for every program or every department. Design selection and research techniques depend upon the intended uses to be made of the study, the decisions that have to be made, the information needs of sponsors, and the constraints and limitations of the agency.

REFERENCES

[1] Tony Tripodi, Phillip Fellin, and Irwin Epstein, *Social Program Evaluation: Guidelines for Health, Education and Welfare Administrators* (Itasca, Ill.: F. E. Peacock Publishers, 1971), pp. 45–50.

[2] Tourism Outdoor Recreation Planning Committee, *Tourism Outdoor Recreation Planning Study: Information Brief on the Ontario Recreation Survey* (Toronto: The Committee), June 1973, 11 pp. Mimeographed.

[3] W. R. D. Sewell, John David, A. D. Scott, and D. W. Ross, *Guide to Benefit-Cost Analysis* (Ottawa: Information Canada, 1965), p. 7.

[4] C. West Churchman, Russell Ackoff, and Leonard Arnoff. *Introduction to Operations Research* (New York: John Wiley and Sons, 1957).

[5] The Leisure Studies Data Bank of the Department of Recreation, University of Waterloo, is a library of computerized numeric data concerning the leisure behavior of various populations. The bank makes it possible for researchers to conduct secondary statistical analyses upon large-scale samples. The original data have been collected by various federal or provincial departments or ministries or by private research organizations under public contract. Thus, all the raw data in the data bank are in the public domain. Subsequently, members of the faculty established liaision with various federal and provincial organizations which collect leisure-related data. Since the University of Waterloo is one of the foremost North American educational institutions engaged in the study of computer science, it seemed logical to concentrate on large-scale studies using the advanced computer technology provided at the university. As a consequence, the department of recreation is now the custodian of a number of "data files" which are available to the university

community and others who wish to conduct secondary analysis of
these studies and engage in research related to the study of leisure.
[6] Novia Carter and Brian Wharf, *Evaluating Social Development Programs* (Parkdale, Ontario: Canadian Council on Social Development, 1973), pp. 26–28.
[7] Throughout much of organized recreation, the term "special populations" has replaced "therapeutic recreation" since the latter referred to leisure programs in homes, hospitals, and other medically oriented settings. Proponents of the special populations usage see this as a more encompassing frame of reference. They include in addition to medical settings, programs in psychiatric, geriatric, and correctional institutions.
[8] Donald T. Campbell, "Reformers as Experiments," in Elmer L. Struening and Marcia Guttentag, *Handbook of Evaluation Research*, vol. 1 (Beverly Hills, Cal.: Sage Publications, 1975), p. 95.
[9] Blaine R. Worthen and James R. Sanders, *Educational Evaluation: Theory and Practice* (Worthington, Ohio: Charles A. Jones Publishing Co., 1973), pp. 210–15.

PART
THREE

THE PRODUCT OF
EVALUATION IN
RECREATION AND PARKS

8

RESULTS OF EVALUATION RESEARCH

It should be clear from the preceding chapters that one of the major weaknesses in recreation and park programs is the obvious need for better performance measures. No matter who makes the decisions, effective delivery of recreation services depends upon measures of achievement. At the local level, municipalities and institutions need ways to gauge the success of different services in order to provide the best ones. Whether recreation programs are sponsored by public or private sectors, each needs performance measures to assess the effectiveness of programs being sponsored.

Relatively lilttle effort has gone into devising measures of performance despite their importance. In addition to a lack of effort, many recreation and park administrators do not have, or will not spend, the time required to undertake the intellectual challenge of the task. Most recreation officials apparently accept uniform standards by which to compare their programs rather than develop individual measures of performance. However, these standards have been criticized for their inability to discriminate between differences in local communities. More sensitive and less quantitatively biased measures that reflect not only the individual differences of participants, but also the unique quality and character of each sponsoring department or agency are necessary.

PERFORMANCE MEASURES

Two general rules can be suggested for developing performance measures in recreation and park programs. First, single measures of service performance should be avoided since they usually lead to distortion, ineffectiveness, and similar undesirable results. Departments cannot be judged on acreage to population standards alone, or staff to participant ratios alone, or numbers of participants served by the program. Multiple measures reflect multiple objectives and avoid distortion. One should imagine recreation programs developing a variety of measures of leisure status and participant satisfaction. In addition, because programs vary in length, performance measures must assess programs over differing time spans. For some purposes measures without weights would be sufficient. For example, in a skill acquisition program, a recreation leader could simply make available a cumulative list of component skills or performance measures and let participants choose their own weighting systems. On the other hand, for an in-service training program for playground leaders, it would be necessary to assign weights to the various success measures being used because of the diversity of playground programs. Those activities that are more essential to program success carry greater priority. If several measures are combined, the weights may not be significant, as long as no single measure is allowed to dominate or distort the reward system.

The second general rule is that performance measures must reflect the complexity of the program. If absolute levels of performance are rewarded, then departments may select only those programs that are relatively easy to conduct, or those with a high success potential. To avoid distortions, recreation program measures always must consider the difficulty of the task. In general, measures of change are better than measures of absolute level, but even the latter approach may not solve the problem. It may be easier to significantly change the performance behavior of normal children than emotionally disturbed ones, or to reduce the social isolation of ambulatory aged than chronically ill ones.

How to determine performance measures is not an easy task. Nonetheless, it is unlikely there will be improved recreation programming (or knowledge that it has improved) until sustained efforts are made to determine performance measures suitable for judging program effectiveness. Performance measures in recreation are not ends in themselves. They are prerequisites to finding more effective means of delivering recreation services and to constructing incentives that will encourage their use. The results of evaluation research efforts depend largely on how findings are written and communicated to decision makers.

WRITING THE EVALUATION REPORT

Once the evaluator has collected and analyzed the data, the next step is to write the evaluation report. Like the results of other research investigations, evaluation studies should present, in logical fashion, the results that prove or disprove the hypotheses. In some cases, however, the written report may be somewhat different from the conventional research study. Evaluators should refrain from using unfamiliar jargon or language. Technical data or terms often used by social researchers discourage the report from being read. The majority of readers cannot or will not read the entire report, so it is wise for the evaluator to prepare a brief summary of the conclusions and recommendations. An interesting summary may encourage one to read the entire report. As in business reports, the evaluator should begin with a proposition, develop a precis, and upon completion of the report, furnish an abstract.

How should the report be written? The outline presented in Figure 8.1 is a modification of one suggested by the U.S. Department of Health, Education and Welfare.[1] As indicated above, a summary of findings and major recommendations should precede the body of the report. The purpose of the summary then is to provide an overview of the study.

The second section of the report should present factual information on where the study was conducted; provide information on socioeconomic data that relates to the community and its residents; present an overview of the department's organization, budgetary situation, and historical background; and specify which program decisions led to initiation of the evaluation study.

The third section of the report deals with the specification of program inputs. The purpose, philosophy, goals, and objectives of the department and its program should be presented as a basis for measurement of effectiveness. The report should indicate the number and kind of resources—that is, staff, budget, equipment, and facilities—that have been allocated to the program operation. It should provide information on the details of the program—answer the classical rhetorical questions of who, how, where, what, when, and why. In addition, the study should attempt to determine the extent of community participation in the planning and operation of the program, and the extent to which residents now participate and have done so in the past. Finally, the report must provide measurement information in order to provide comparative data, or provide a rationale for differences in performance measures.

The fourth section details what the evaluation expects to accomplish by listing clear, specific, and measureable evaluation objectives. It then provides data on participant choice, such as who was chosen, how, and why. The study presents the methods and techniques used to measure change or outcome, then it reports the statistical analysis of the data. The study's findings and conclusions are then presented and compared with the causes and effects of the program. In other words,

SECTION I.   THE SUMMARY
SECTION II.   CONTEXT OF THE EVALUATION
   A. The Community
     1. Population Patterns of the Community
     2. Economic Patterns of the Community
   B. The Recreation and Park Department
     1. Organization of the Department
     2. Financial Status of the Department
   C. Special Factors
     1. Historical Background
     2. Questions or Decisions About the Program
   D. Rationale for the Evaluation
SECTION III. PROGRAM SPECIFICATION
   A. Philosophy and Purpose of the Department
     1. Departmental Goals
     2. Program Objectives
   B. Scope of the Program
   C. Personnel
   D. Program Procedures
     1. Organizational Details
     2. Activities or Services
     3. Equipment and Facilities
     4. Community Involvement
   E. Participants
     1. Previous Recreation Opportunities
     2. Participation Patterns
   F. Budget
   G. Present Basis for Judging Quality
SECTION IV.   REPORTING THE EVALUATION
   A. Evaluation Objectives
   B. Participant Sample
   C. Methodology and Procedures
   D. Presentation and Analysis of Data
   E. Findings and Conclusions
SECTION V.   RECOMMENDATIONS

FIGURE 3.2   Outline for an Evaluation Report

have the stated objectives of the program been accomplished, and, if so, to what degree?

In the final section, the evaluator prepares specific recommendations based upon the study conclusions. The evaluator's analysis should provide the decision maker with the necessary information about what might be expected or desirable if the program were to be repeated, continued, or modified.

COMMUNICATING THE RESULTS
OF EVALUATION

The results of recreation evaluation studies must be communicated as broadly as possible, not only to the sponsoring agency, but to others involved with the department or program in order to make them more accountable to the public and more effective to participants. This statement may appear too idealistic since the majority of evaluation studies done in recreation and parks are seldom implemented. Most program evaluation reports are generally circulated to only a few members of the department or agency. They are often numbered to maximize internal control, and if the report is seen as derogatory, it may well wind up on the shelf, uncirculated, unseen, and unused. Rarely are the important evaluation results communicated to the field by articles in professional journals or books. Often, the sponsoring agency, as a condition of conducting the evaluation will swear the evaluator to absolute secrecy in regard to the study results. At other times, the design or procedures are so poorly conceived or carried out that the study fails to live up to the standards of good scholarship. One of the major inhibiting factors to increasing the body of knowledge in recreation and parks is the lack of available information on such research as program evaluation.

UTILIZING EVALUATION RECOMMENDATIONS

After the evaluation study has been completed, the decision maker must decide what to do with it. The evaluator may again be called upon to answer any questions the decision maker may have. Tripodi et al. suggests four such questions:

1. What do the findings mean in terms of the program objectives?
2. How can the findings be utilized to bring about changes in a particular program?
3. What implications would the implementation of findings have for the overall program?
4. What next steps are necessary, such as new evaluation efforts, implementation of change, or movement to new stages of program development.[2]

Often, these questions arise from the presentation of findings, but are not specifically dealt with in the recommendations section. The evaluator must interpret the findings to the decision maker. If the report is to be presented to the City Council or Recreation Commission or Board, the evaluator may well be asked to either make the presentation or assist the administrator as a resource consultant. This is the positive side of evaluation implementation. There are a number of circumstances however that will determine whether or not the study will be implemented.

The utilization and implementation of evaluation recommendations can be greatly enhanced from discussions held with the administrator and staff, prior to making the recommendations formal. The greater the degree of involvement by agency personnel in the interpretation of results and formulation of recommendations, the greater the likelihood that the recommendations will be accepted and implemented. A common error evaluators often make is to suggest program changes without first discussing them with those staff members who will be most affected. Prior consultation is desirable since it can lessen resistance to change, and the change itself may be modified based upon pertinent staff information. Consultation however does not mean that the staff will like or agree with the proposed change, but only that they might understand the basis on which these changes are suggested. Ultimately, as with any evaluation study, the outcome of the recommendations are likely to be whatever the administrator and staff assign to them. The results of recreation evaluation studies will have little effect on recreation programs until the study results are understood and accepted by the program staff.

Another reason that evaluation studies often fail to produce the desired results is that the information obtained from the study does not match the information needs of administrators. If the administrator wants to improve the program and all the evaluator suggests is that the program produced changes in attitudes or skills, there is no basis for program improvement. Evaluations, if they are to be successful must *identify* the specific information needs of administrators, and if they are to be utilized, they must *produce* this specific information. Most administrators expect an evaluation study to be useful. A primary source of reluctance may be the skepticism of an administrator regarding the "practical value" of such research. Although most recreation and park practitioners recognize the need to assess the measure of how well they are doing, the process of being compared or measured is often threatening.

According to Edward Suchman, two factors affect the utilization of evaluation studies: (1) program and organizational forces and (2) public reaction.[3] A primary instinct of organizations is self-preservation. Evaluations that suggest change or question the basic purpose of organizations often are met with reluctance or hostility. Those activities that have been in existence the longest are often the most difficult to change. For example, if bingo has been a Friday evening activity in a nursing home for a period of time, and the evaluator suggests that it be played on Tuesdays or that it be replaced by another activity, there is often such a cry of outrage that any change becomes impossible to effect. To overcome potential resistance to change, the evaluator must make allies of both the staff and the participants. It is also well to remember that gradual changes are often more palatable than sudden and dramatic changes

Just as organizations are reluctant to effect changes in recreation programs, so too are those who regularly participate in the program. Once people have become accustomed to an activity program, they are likely to resist the thought of losing it, even if it is ineffective. Studies of compensatory education for children have demonstrated that no matter the type of program, or the actual results, parents are enthusiastic about it.[4] Recreation activities like basketball, baseball, and football, even though professional knowledge suggests little carryover value in them, continue to exist because of public demand. Traditional playgrounds have been severely criticized by psychologists, landscape architects, and educators, but nevertheless they are still being constructed in every state and province because of demand. The evaluator must be aware of tradition, culture, mores, and behavior within the community under study if recommendations are to be accepted and implemented. The evaluator may take one of two positions: give them more of what they want by recommending continuation or an increase of the current program, even though the program can become stagnant; or to suggest alternatives that have the potential to enrich and expand the program. The second alternative is more difficult since these evaluation recommendations may meet with resistance. However, the evaluator has the responsibility to provide the sponsor with the best possible information that is available as the result of the program assessment.

The results of evaluation studies do not always indicate clearly how improvements in recreation programs are to be accomplished. Occasionally, the outcome of the study can say little more than that the objectives of the activity are not being met. However, administrators and program personnel realize that some activities are more successful than others, some leaders are more effective than others, or that one group may be doing better than another. Indicators may be present that the evaluator has failed to identify, so when this situation occurs, program personnel must be consulted to determine why a particular program did not live up to its expectations.

Contributions of Evaluation

Evaluation studies point out strengths and weaknesses of program activities, but often only suggest vague or inconclusive reasons for the condition. Recreators must realize that evaluation studies cannot give all the answers. However, such studies can contribute to:

1. Support for those agency personnel who seek program improvements.
2. Generate interest in the program outside the agency itself.
3. Increase awareness and publicity about the program.
4. Suggest changes in the agencies' mission or goals.
5. Reexamine and identify appropriate program objectives.

The most practical benefit of recreation program evaluation is in its ability to reinforce and support the view of those agency personnel who feel that changes in program operation are necessary. By providing "hard" data that certain activities are ineffectively meeting their objectives, evaluation studies provide ammunition to reformers both within and outside the recreation and park department. If repeated evaluations point out the same basic program weaknesses, these findings may influence the most hardened administrators.

Responsibilities of Evaluators

Recreation program evaluation also may suggest alternatives to current program operation practices. This is especially true if the evaluator has professional experience in the field, and is respected for other work. If personally known by the sponsoring organization, the evaluator may be given a freer hand and greater latitude in offering alternative program recommendations. However, the evaluator must suggest only those alternatives that are based upon the collected data rather than rely on unsubstantiated, past experience. If recommendations are based upon experience, the evaluator must inform program administrators of the basis for these recommendations. A second responsibility of the evaluator who offers program alternatives is to try to determine the outcome(s) of these changes and how they might affect the agency. The decision maker then has some idea of the implications involved in alternative program activities. It is essential that the decision maker be apprised of all the potential possibilities, both good and bad, before the decision is made.

Political Considerations

Some recreation program decisions are political, rather than technical, and evaluation results that do not correspond with political realities faced by administrators are not likely to be implemented. For example, if a new government has been elected to office on the strength of their commitment to reduce taxes, an evaluative recommendation to increase full-time program staff or to expand the number of tennis courts would probably not be received favorably. The implications of this fact cannot be ignored if program evaluation in recreation and parks is to be recognized as a legitimate activity, and to be continued as a viable technique for trained evaluators. Although there have been significant advances in evaluation research methodology, little investigation has been conducted on the political considerations that may be involved with public agency program evaluation. The power of a political jurisdiction may lead to compromise between the actual and the ideal in recommendation implementation. There should be no misunderstanding or naivete with regard to influence of political pressure. Where politics mitigate against the evaluator conducting an objective, valid, and reliable study, it is best to not undertake the project. On the other hand, if these constraints do not exist, and the evaluator has freedom to conduct the study but meets resistance only at the final recommendations stage, compromise would be welcome. Proposals for *dramatic* change might have to be modified to allow for *gradual* change. In the final analysis, the question must be raised: Are the program and its participants better served by changes made over a period of time, or by no changes at all? Ultimately, if the program has proved to be ineffective, the answer becomes obvious.

CHOICES OF RECOMMENDATIONS

Once the evaluation study has been completed and the recommendations for change have been proposed, the administrator must decide which one, or how many, of the recommendations to implement. Selection criteria are usually based upon the factors of utility, practicality, priority, compatability, and time.

Evaluation recommendations that are usable and practical almost always are implemented. Unfortunately, evaluators do not always recognize that there are certain limitations in recreation program operation, the most important being budgetary constraints. If the evaluator recommends construction of a performing arts center, and the municipality has already reached its bond indebtedness limit, this recommendation becomes impractical and therefore useless. On the other hand, if a recommendation suggests redeployment of existing staff members, and one activity will not suffer but another will be more effective, the recommendation becomes both practical and useful.

The third implementation factor is priority, or the relative importance of different recommendations. The administrator must judge program priorities. Even if the administrator is convinced that all recommendations are appropriate, some will obviously be more central to the goals and objectives of the department than others. The evaluator may be asked to assist the administrator and staff to prioritize the recommendations, based upon their relative importance to the program operation.

In some cases there may be incompatibilities among the proposed recommendations. For example, there is little compatibility between the following two recommendations:

1. It is recommended that decentralization of recreation programs and services take place in order to strengthen neighborhood recreation councils.
2. It is recommended that in order to decrease the contract costs of goods and supplies, that all purchases of recreation equipment and supplies be made by the central recreation and parks office.

If two goals of the department are to encourage community participation at the neighborhood level, and another is to encourage creativity and innovation in programs at the local level, then these recommendations conflict with each other. Certainly, central purchasing should reduce costs and provide a more uniform accounting system, but it may well discourage program decentralization and innovation at the local level by reducing the neighborhood expenditure flexibility. Which recommendation then becomes more important? Evaluators must be aware of potential conflicts among recommendations, and be prepared to offer alternatives that will reduce or eliminate this conflict.

The final factor is the time span necessary to implement the suggested recommendations. Some may be affected immediately, others may take a few weeks or months, while a few may take years to implement. Which of the recommendations then become more important? Recreation and park administrators usually respond to immediate demands quickly, while long-range needs often are unmet. Decision makers prefer immediate answers to immediate questions and problems, and just as often respond to the budget cycle in implementing evaluation recommendations. It is incumbent upon evaluators to impress on administrators the value of moving toward implementation of long-range recommendations, since foresight is better than hindsight in anticipating potential program problems. Planning for change is far better than waiting until change occurs, and an immediate decision must be made without the benefit of investigation and analysis.

Evaluation research literature suggests that the utilization phase is the fourth item in a continuum of: (1) research, (2) development, (3) dissemination, and (4) utilization. Davis and Salasin describe five continuum models that are in use today:

(a) The first is the research, development, and diffusion model. This model assumes there is a relatively passive target audience of consumers which will accept an innovation if it is delivered through a suitable medium, in the right way, at the right time. It calls for a rational sequence of activities from research to development to packaging before dissemination takes place. It assumes large-scale planning, and requires a division of labor and a separation of roles and functions. Evaluation is particularly emphasized in this model, in which there is a high initial development cost and which anticipates a high payoff in terms of the quantity and quality of long-range benefit through its capacity to reach a mass audience.

(b) The second is the social interaction model, which is more sensitive to the complex and intricate set of human relationships, substructures, and processes that are involved in the dissemination phase, and which stresses the importance of face-to-face contacts. This model implies that a user can hold a variety of positions in the communication network, and that people tend to adopt and maintain attitudes and behavior which they perceive as normative for their psychological reference group. The size of the adopting group is basically irrelevant in this model, which follows essentially the process stages of knowledge and research diffusion, with appropriate influencing strategies used at each stage.

(c) Third is the problem solving model, which starts with the user's needs as a beginning point for research, with diagnosis as an essential first step in the search for solutions. The outside helper, or change agent, in this model, is largely non-directive, mainly guiding the potential user through his own problem-solving processes and encouraging him to utilize internal resources. The model assumes that self-initiated and directed change has the firmest motivation and hence the best prospect for maintenance.

(d) In the fourth model, the planned change model, information is considered useful only if it leads to action, and is shared between the change agent and the client. The assumptive basis of this model is that change occurs through a consciously controlled sequential

and continuous process of data generalization, planning, and implementation. The changes made need to be stabilized and supported.
(e) The fifth model is the action research model. *Although similar in some respects to the problem-solving and planned change models, it is most distinctive in emphasizing the development of research within the organization. The type of research and its methodology are influenced by its concurrent conduct with the ongoing activity of the organization. The results of the research, while primarily intended for the organization itself, may prove useful to others and contribute to behavioral science itself. The model assumes the action research to be a continuous process of research, action, evaluation, and more research.* [5]

It is likely that when choosing any one of these models, the recreation administrator will have to rely on a specialist. An example of the research, development, and diffusion model might be a broadly based, national program such as scouting, which has recently dropped the prefix "boy" from its title in order to accommodate other target populations. The social interaction model might be utilized in revising a recreation and park curriculum at a large university and sifting through the process of committee decisions at different levels in the structure. Examples of the problem-solving model can be found in therapeutic institutions where individuals try to meet their own leisure needs. The planned change model is most appropriate to municipal recreation programs, but note that action, rather than reaction, is the essential element. Most bureaucratic institutions do not fall under this category since the role of institutions is generally not to anticipate or plan for change, but rather to regulate the rate of change. The action research model might relate to an agency or organization whose primary purpose is to conduct research. In addition, social action programs, such as recreation and parks, committed to ongoing research within their programs would fit in this model category. However, the essential element in the action model is the continuous reliance upon the principles of scientific investigation in order to test, refine, actuate, and evaluate action programs.

CONCLUSION

Evaluation research studies of recreation and park programs run the risk of one or two types of failure. The first type—a technical failure of the research design—results when the specific program objective

definitions and program performance measurements do not correspond to the actual program goals. Such studies provide incomplete
accounts of program effectiveness. As a result, administrators and staff
who are satisfied with the program may claim the study has underes-
timated or misinterpreted the program's purpose. The second type of
failure is political in nature. If the study indicates that the recreation
program is a failure, or has little effect on participants, the findings
may be unacceptable to the sponsoring agency. If administrators have
oversold the program or have a major role in its outcome, they may
not accept the fact that the evaluation finds fault with the program.

Evaluation research studies of recreation and park programs will
continue to be a difficult and sometimes futile undertaking for two
reasons. First, evaluators attempt to focus on program outcomes that
are either minimal or secondary to specific objectives, as perceived
by administrators and staff. Also, recreation and park administrators
have a significant political stake in any evaluation of program effectiveness. Evaluation studies can determine and measure effectiveness
best when program objectives are clear, specific, and measureable,
and the studies are geared to investigate reasonably well-defined problems. Evaluation results will have a far greater impact on decision
making when administrators and other policy makers insist less on
findings that are acceptable to them, and more on understanding
those elements that determine program effectiveness. Only when evaluation studies are commissioned, conducted, and implemented with
the aim of improving program effectiveness can recreation and park
departments continue to offer citizens the best possible programs, at
the least possible cost.

Although the situation is not promising, it should not deter evaluation studies from being undertaken. What it does suggest is that
research should be better designed to match more closely the information needs of the decision maker and the nature and scope of the
program under study. In order to establish the proper ground rules
prior to the start of the study, both the administrator and the evaluator
must be fully aware of the possible political and technical problems.
In some cases, rather than emphasize the effect of the program on
achieving specific objectives, the objectives themselves should be
assessed in terms of their appropriateness in meeting community
needs and interests. However, fairly well-defined programs in recreation can continue to be evaluated in conventional ways, with the
emphasis being placed on cause (program) versus effect (objective
attainment). Ultimately, whatever the rationale, or the design chosen
for an evaluation study, it must be recognized that policy and problem
analysis may need to be included. This element is essential since what
administrators can accomplish often is directly related to the character

and quality of the policy-making process that led to the establishment of the programs initially.

SUMMARY

The preceding chapters have pointed out the increasing need for recreation and park program evaluation. It is encouraging to note that there has been a large volume of work devoted to this topic, especially in assessing the effects of programs dealing with mental health, poverty, and related domestic problems. Some promising approaches and models have been developed that may, with modification, be applied to the delivery of leisure services. To carefully select a model(s) that is appropriate to the program under investigation the evaluator has to consider several variables. The use of differential evaluation, using multiple measures, offers the most potential to recreation and park assessment. In addition, evaluation should be conducted on an ongoing basis, rather than a "one-shot" assessment. The question of who will conduct the evaluation study depends upon the experience and skills of the evaluator, the level of the evaluation, and the stage of program development reached by the sponsoring agency.

Evaluation of recreation and park programs is an activity that poses many problems or obstacles. Administrators often approach evaluation on an impressionistic or instinctive basis, and they are often reluctant to make the investment necessary to assess their programs objectively, validly, and reliably. Problems of design and measurement severely restrict the ability to reach substantiated conclusions. Poor communication or hostility between the evaluator and agency staff members can minimize the collection of essential information. Results of evaluation studies may be so narrow and restrictive that they offer program administrators little or no practical benefits. Alternately, administrators may ignore or disregard highly pertinent findings of evaluation studies. These and other obstacles often hinder the decision whether or not to evaluate a program.

However, there are a number of compelling reasons for conducting evaluation studies of recreation and park programs. All levels of government spend a substantial portion of their operating and capital budgets on leisure services. At the same time, a number of highly questionable recreation and park programs that have never had a program effectiveness evaluation continue to be offered because of tradition, blind acceptance, or historical artifact. Increases in program costs usually far outweigh improvements in services. There appears to be agreement that leisure services must be strengthened and improved, especially in light of demands for accountability and increased productivity. At the same time, budgets have been frozen or reduced. These facts place a heavy responsibility on administrators who will have to make a number of difficult program decisions. Since this improvement must result from rational methods of planning, evaluation then becomes essential to program operation. This is especially true of recreation programs where the results are not obvious such as special events and other one-time program efforts. Therefore, evaluation studies are needed to produce precise information on program effectiveness.

Faced with an increased demand for more effective recreation and park programs to meet the leisure needs of contemporary society, evaluation research becomes increasingly more important as a source of knowledge and direction. It suggests those programs which work and recommends alternatives to better policy formulation and program operation. It helps to identify methods and techniques within program activities that either assist or detract from achieving specific objectives. Finally, evaluation provides data that can reduce program uncertainties and help clarify the gains and losses that different decisions incur. It allows decision makers to apply their values and preferences more accurately, with more concrete information regarding the tradeoffs that alternative decisions involve.

Program evaluation must become an integral part of the leisure-service delivery system. Program managers and administrators must recognize that recreation and park services depend upon the organization and management of resources and activities. Precisely because evaluation research is the study of the relationship between planned activity and desired outcomes, it is obvious that evaluation studies become an essential management tool. Recognized as such, evaluation research can add immeasurably not only to the planning process in recreation and parks, but also to assisting leisure service personnel in increasing their potential for achieving program success.

REFERENCES

[1] Office of Education, U.S. Department of Health, Education, and Welfare, *Preparing Evaluation Reports: A Guide for Authors* (Washington, D.C.: U.S. Government Printing Office, 1970), p. ii.
[2] Tony Tripodi, Phillip Fellin, and Irwin Epstein, *Social Program Evaluation: Guidelines for Health, Education, and Welfare Administrators* (Itasca, Ill.: F. E. Peacock Publishers, 1971), p. 135.
[3] Edward A. Suchman, *Evaluative Research: Principles and Practice in*

Public Service and Social Action Programs (New York: Russell Sage Foundation, 1967), pp. 164-65.

[4] Edward L. McDill, Mary S. McDill, and J. Tillman Sprehe, *Strategies for Success in Compensatory Education: An Appraisal of Evaluation Research* (Baltimore: Johns Hopkins Press, 1969), pp. 43-44.

[5] Howard R. Davis and Susan E. Salasin, "The Utilization of Evaluation," in Elmer L. Struening, and Marcia Guttentag, eds., *Handbook of Evaluation Research*, vol. 1 (Beverly Hills, Cal.: Sage Publications, 1975), pp. 628-29.

APPENDIX

Readers who wish to locate the most current and timely information on evaluation practices and evaluation research can refer to the following *quarterly* publications:

Evaluation in the Health Professions. Empirical Publishers, Inc., Post Office Box 13345, Baltimore, Maryland 21203.

Evaluation and Program Planning. Pergamon Press, Inc., Maxwell House, Fairview Park, Elmsford, New York 10523.

Evaluation Quarterly. Sage Publications, Inc., Post Office Box 776, Beverly Hills, California 90213.

For readers who wish to pursue in greater detail the purpose, process, or product of evaluation in recreation and parks, the following list of titles and annotations is provided. Almost 50 such references are suggested, which cover a wide range of evaluation material. References are provided not only on the evaluation of programs, but also on the assessment of personnel and resources in recreation and parks.

Ad Hoc Committee on Recreation for the Disadvantaged. *Recreation for the Disadvantaged: A Report of Selected Public Recreation Services for Target Communities in Westchester County.* White Plains, N.Y., Westchester Council of Social Agencies, November 1970. Mimeographed. This committee report sought ways in which to provide more effective public and voluntary recreation services to disadvantaged residents of a county in New York State. The committee used a statistical review technique to assess recreation opportunity within two geographic areas of the county.

Auckland Regional Authority. *Recreation Patterns in Auckland.* Auckland, New Zealand, The Authority, 1971. This study attempted to identify Auckland's recreation patterns and the need for further involvement. Questionnaires were employed, and the results were grouped under five main headings: sports and games, fitness and personal grooming, social activities, the arts, and hobbies. For each activity there were figures on both actual and desired participation. From these figures, predictions were made about the current appeal and likely future demand for activity.

Berryman, Doris L. *Recommended Standards with Evaluative Criteria for Recreation Services in Residential Institutions.* New York, School of Education, New York University, 1971. The purpose of this study was to suggest standards and evaluative criteria for hospitals and other institutions in evaluating recreation services provided to residents. Six categories are proposed: philosophy and goals, administration, personnel, programming, resources and equipment, and evaluation, including research. A rating scale was developed that assessed the degree to which each criterion and subcriterion was met.

Booth, Graham, et al. *The Resolve Report: A Recreation Study of Lincoln Village.* Waterloo, Ontario, Lincoln Village Community Association, n.d. The report assessed the recreational needs of the residents within one geographic region of Waterloo. A community survey intended to: determine how residents are currently using their leisure time, what they will do in the future, inventory leadership potential, analyze open space and citizen perception of its use, and assess recreation needs of future residents.

Brown, Robert and Donald Fisk. *Recreation Planning and Analysis in Local Government.* Washington, D.C., The Urban Institute, June 1973. A reprinted publication from the *Municipal Year Book* which presents data on city, county, and regional agency recreation planning in the United States. The survey includes data on the number, type, and location of planning within local government agencies; the number, type and jurisdiction of recreation planning; subjects of special studies (including evaluation); and analysis conducted within each setting.

Bureau of Outdoor Recreation. *How Effective Are Your Recreation Services.* Washington, D.C., U.S. Department of the Interior, April 1973. This report presents a suggested set of measurements and procedures for collecting recreation program effectiveness data. The major data collection technique proposed is a citizen survey which attempts to assess the enjoyability, attractiveness, accessibility, safety, and variety of recreation programs.

Capling, R. G., ed. *Shared Decision-Making in Recreation Programs in Canada.* Kitchner, Ontario, Recreation Administration Program, Conestoga College, 1970. The study assessed participatory planning by citizens in decision making with respect to recreation programs throughout Canada. This field study employed questionnaires, interviews, and case studies from six provinces within the country.

Christensen, Kathleen. *Social Impacts of Land Development: An Initial Approach for Estimating Impacts on Neighborhood Usages and Perceptions.* Washington, D.C., The Urban Institute, September 1976. This report establishes a series of impact measures that can be used by local governments to assess the off-site effects of proposed land development. It also describes various procedures for determining impact measurements. Included in the report are measures for determining social impact of proposed recreation resource develop-

ments. A second forthcoming report will assess the applicability of
these measures to local land use and decision making.

Cicchetti, Charles J., and V. Kerry Smith. "Congestion, Optimal Use
and Benefit Estimation: A Case Study of Wilderness Recreation," in
James G. Abert and Murray Kamrass, eds. *Social Experiments and
Social Program Evaluation.* Cambridge, Mass., Ballinger Publishing
Company, 1974. pp. 80–91. An attempt to develop a system by which
to evaluate qualitative factors of recreation—for example, an economic analysis ascribing monetary value to recreation participant
experiences. In order to solve the deterioration of recreation resources due to participant congestion, a model is used to estimate
and utilize individual willingness-to-pay functions in order that optimal use and net benefits of the resources may be derived.

Community Programmes Branch. *Evaluation.* Toronto, Ontario Department of Education, n.d. This pamphlet describes the need for,
and steps in conducting program evaluation. It suggests how to
devise a rating scale and explains principles of program observation.

Community Renewal Program. *Recreation Facilities in New York City:
A Method of Assigning Budgetary Priorities.* New York, City Planning
Commission, November 1968. Mimeographed. This report proposes
a method for allocating recreation capital funds to city areas based
upon relative needs. The methodology involves compiling the number of recreation resources within neighborhoods, then establishing
a city-wide average of these resources. The second part of the study
gathered data on income levels within each neighborhood, again
establishing a city-wide average income level. Income was compared
against number of resources, and budgetary priorities were established according to need levels.

Department of Local Affairs and Development. *Recreation Site Evaluation Development Series.* Madison, Wisconsin, State Division of
Economic Development, Bureau of Recreation, 1968. This report
proposes methods for evaluating potential sites for both public and
private outdoor recreation agencies. It is intended to help the de-
veloper make planning decisions with respect to assessing recreation lands.

Division of Municipal Recreation and Adult Education. *A Handbook of
Information: Program Evaluation.* Milwaukee, Wisconsin, Milwaukee
Public Schools, n.d. This handbook is basically a reporting system
for data gathered on the effectiveness of the recreation program.
Methods for gathering quantitative department data on program
attendance, service statistics, and seasonal program budgets are
given. Qualitative data gathered through patron and organization
questionnaires and interviews, staff observation visits, and employee conferences are detailed.

Economics Research Associates. *Evaluation of Public Willingness to Pay User Charges for Use of Outdoor Recreation Areas and Facilities.* Prepared for the U.S. Department of the Interior, Bureau of Outdoor Recreation. Washington, D.C., Superintendent of Documents, October 1976. This study attempted to develop a data base as to the current fee policies of government agencies, fee levels in comparable public and private areas, and public willingness to pay for recreation services. A comparison technique was employed to assess user charges at public and private areas. Data were drawn from interviews and household surveys.

Fisk, Donald M. and Cynthia A. Lancer. *Equality and Distribution of Recreation Services: A Case Study of Washington, D.C.* Washington, D.C., The Urban Institute, July 1974. A comparison evaluation study that measures the equality of recreation services within two neighboring geographic areas. Capital expenditures, operating expenditures, quantity of participation opportunities, quality of opportunities, and utilization rates of each area were examined and compared for differences.

Governor's Committee on Recreation. *Recreation in Indiana: A Critical Evaluation of the Recreation Facilities and Leadership Available to the Citizens of the 92 Counties Comprising the State.* Indianapolis, Indiana State Board of Health, n.d. An older study that attempted to identify and compare recreation facilities and leadership against national standards for adequacy. Two schedules were developed: an inventory of facilities and leadership available, and an opinionnaire completed by citizens to record their attitudes toward the adequacy of recreation facilities within their geographic area.

Gunn, C. A. and A. J. Worms. *Evaluating and Developing Tourism.* College Station, Texas, Agricultural Experiment Station, Texas A & M University, July 1973. This study attempted to assess the experience survey as a method of obtaining citizen input prior to planning tourism development. The experience survey is based upon the assumption that certain individuals (due to occupation, training, and experience) may reflect the collective opinions of many other people they are acquainted with. By employing the opinions and knowledge of these individuals, a valuable cross-section of tourism planning information may be obtained from a given geographic area.

Hatry, Harry P. and Diana R. Dunn. *Measuring the Effectiveness of Local Government Services: Recreation.* Washington, D.C., The Urban Institute, 1971. This study presents a variety of new recreation program effectiveness measures such as participation patterns, accessibility, crowdedness, variety, safety, attractiveness, and citizen satisfaction with recreation resources. Also, indirect recreation effects such as crime, delinquency, health, and local economy are identified. Data collection procedures for each measure are indicated, with emphasis on agency response.

Heit, Michael J. *Girl Guides: An Analysis of "Guiding in Ontario—An Opinionnaire."* Toronto, Research Branch, Ontario Ministry of Community and Social Services, December 1974. Photocopied. The purpose of this study was to determine the opinions and beliefs of adult membership of all levels within Ontario's Girl Guide Program. The opinionnaire sought to determine the members' perceptions of the organization, the present needs of the organization, and possible future directions of guiding.

Leichester, J.B. *Winnipeg Parks and Recreation Study.* Winnipeg, Manitoba, Parks and Recreation Committee, 1967. This study surveyed and collected existing data pertaining to parks and recreation and investigated structure, organization and administration, personnel, program, facilities, relationships, and population. Presentation of present conditions, appraisal of all categories, recommendations to meet needs and problems of recreation, and guidelines for implementation were included. Methodology consisted of questionnaires, interviews, and bivariate correlations.

Mannell, Roger C. *Evaluation Resources for Recreation Programs.* Wolfeville, Nova Scotia, Acadia University, 1977. Mimeographed. A valuable reference source of evaluation techniques and references first compiled for a workshop on evaluating community recreation services sponsored by the Recreation Association of Nova Scotia, the Nova Scotia Department of Recreation and the Center of Leisure Studies, Acadia University.

McLean, Christine and Dennis Hermanson. *Leisure Services: The Measurement of Program Performance.* Nashville, Tenn., Metropolitan Department of Parks and Recreation, 1974. A local evaluation study based upon many of the factors from the Hatry and Dunn evaluation model, that included such factors as staff competence, supervision, program cost, and variety. Essentially it was a citizen survey of departmental program effectiveness.

National Recreation and Park Association. *A Comprehensive Study of Parks and Recreation for Town of Hamburg, New York.* Washington, D.C., The Association, April 1968. A typical community recreation and park study conducted by the Association over the years which included factors influencing recreation, areas and facilities, administration and managing authority, financial resources, and the public recreation program. The study was primarily an inventory of existing and potential resources, but also included appraisals of each element within the survey.

Office of Community Consultation. *Analysis and Design of Public Participation Programme Evaluation in Ontario.* Toronto, Ministry of

Community and Social Services, July 1974. Typewritten. A working paper that attempted to develop a conceptual framework for evaluating citizen (public) participation programs within government services. The model for evaluation of participatory techniques in determining resource allocations is adopted from Tripodi, Fellin, and Epstein, and therefore is essentially an analysis of program efforts, effectiveness, and efficiency.

Office of Recreation and Park Resources. *Recreation Program Appraisal for Skokie Park District, Skokie . . . Illinois.* Urbana-Champaign, University of Illinois, Department of Recreation and Park Administration, March 1970. Typical of the studies conducted by university extension services, this study assesses the entire scope of a recreation and park operating agency. In addition to evaluating the internal structure, financing, relationships, staff and program, these appraisals offer specific recommendations for improvement of service delivery.

Olson, Ernest. *A Model for the Evaluation of Public Leisure Service Programs.* Champaign-Urbana, University of Illinois, June 1972. Ph.D. Dissertation prospectus. Mimeographed. A responsive portrayal evaluation model that devotes greater attention to program activities, audience requirements for information, and different value requirements for information, and different value perspectives than on attention to formal program objectives.

Operations Research, Inc. *Final Report: Analysis of Current and Potential Department Goals, Objectives, and Program Structures.* Toronto, Ontario Department of Lands and Forests, 17 November 1969. An analysis of current and potential department goals, objectives, and program structures as a necessary first step in the development and implementation of a planning-programming-budgeting system (PPBS). It explores the planning and analytical elements of the department along with their legislative mandates and policy issues.

Physical Education Project. *Effective Program Planning and Basic Program Evaluation Criteria.* Toronto, National Council of YMCAs of Canada, July 1973. A self-evaluation checklist for assessing the effectiveness of YMCAs. The evaluation instrument has two forms: a short form to highlight the program operation (monitoring) and a comprehensive form to measure nine program elements: purpose, objectives, leadership, program design, facilities, records, program interpretation, evaluation procedures, and program action.

Recreation and Youth Services Planning Council. *A Behavioral Approach to Evaluating the Effectiveness of Recreation and Youth Services Programs.* Los Angeles, The Council, September 1966. A two-phase study, the first portion produced an instrument by which the effectiveness of social recreation programs could be assessed. The second phase attempted to develop a methodology of assessing participants, activities, and agencies. The aims were: to develop a rationale for selecting relevant dimensions to describe program effectiveness, to develop a scaling procedure to measure these dimensions, and to propose specific hypothetical measurement techniques and procedures to implement the findings. The principle methodology was the development of the behavioral-goals projective survey, based upon Bloom's cognitive domain objective taxonomy.

Recreation and Youth Services Planning Council. *A Comparative Analysis of the Guiding Principles of the Youth Services Program of the Los Angeles City Schools with the Principles Emerging from Recent Recreation Literature.* Los Angeles, The Council, February 1966. This study purpose was to compare the principles of the Los Angeles City Schools Youth Services Program with those emerging from recent recreation literature and suggest implementation of principles stated in the publication, *Goals for American Recreation.* The principle methodology was a content analysis technique of recreation literature, and comparison between this literature and those principles stated in a publication of the American Association for Health, Physical Education, and Recreation.

Recreation Canada. *National Study on the Supply and Demand for Sports and Recreation Facilities: Phase II—Inventory of Socio-Cultural Facilities.* Ottawa, Health and Welfare Canada, 1973. One of a number of national studies on the general concept of supply and demand for recreation facilities, this volume presents the results of a questionnaire intended to measure the site, administration, ownership, typologies, equipment, and programs of sociocultural facilities such as museums, art galleries, auditoriums, theaters, and other recreation resources. This inventory will be compared with future studies of demand in order to provide a data base for recreation planning and policy making at all government levels.

Recreation Resources Center, Extension and Department of Agricultural Economics. *Effect of Selected Socioeconomic Characteristics on Recreation Patterns in Low Income Urban Areas.* Madison, University of Wisconsin, May 1975. Part II of a two-phase study, it determines recreation activities participated in by individuals and families, and identifies meaningful relationships between socioeconomic characteristics and program preferences of participants. The principle methodology was a multiple-classification analysis technique which sought to determine the effect of selected socioeconomic factors against such dependent variables as recreation travel, participation patterns, and recreation expenditures.

Shabman, Leonard A. and Robert J. Kalter. *The Effects of New York*

State Administered Outdoor Recreation Expenditures on the Distribution of Personal Income. Ithaca, New York, Agricultural Experiment Station, Cornell University, September 1969. The study examined the net transfer effects of governmental taxes and expenditures for outdoor recreation. It then analyzed the effects of public investment in outdoor recreation facilities on personal income distribution in terms of the willingness of each income class to pay for the benefits received over time. Equity calculations (benefit) for each income class and coefficients for burden (cost) were determined in order to provide net benefits and net transfer effects.

Siderelis, C. Dimitry. "Factors Influencing Effectiveness in Municipal Recreation Departments," *Journal of Leisure Research*. Vol. 8, No. 4, Fourth Quarter, 1976. pp. 289–91. A research note drawn from the author's doctoral dissertation which sought to measure the influence of several organizational characteristics of municipal recreation departments. Characteristics included need for community recreation service, task orientation by policy body, interdependency between policy body and city government, supervisory competence, department size, administrative size, and organizational structure. Data gathering measures included content analysis, interviews, and questionnaires.

Smith, F. R. *A Study of the Recreation Program*. Lompoc, California, Federal Correctional Institution, April 1971. Mimeographed. An internal program evaluation study that assessed the effectiveness of the indoor and outdoor programs, special events, and recreation facilities for the inmate population. The study focused on past, present, and future program history and potential.

Staley, Edwin J. *An Instrument for Determining Comparative Priority of Need for Neighborhood Recreation Services in the City of Los Angeles*. Los Angeles, Recreation and Youth Services Planning Council, September 1968. Mimeographed. This report describes a need instrument developed to provide a means of better fitting programs to the needs of various neighborhoods served by recreation centers and other facilities. Two indexes were developed: a resource index measuring staff hours, recreation acreage, and number of recreation centers; and a need index measuring youth population, family income, population density, and juvenile delinquency rate. A comparison between the two indexes provided a comparative priority of neighborhood need. The principle methodology for comparison was made by use of C-Scales.

St. Amour, Jeannette. *Nepean Parks and Recreation Program Development Report*. Nepean, Ontario, Parks and Recreation Department, 1975. A program development report whose objectives were to inventory existing programs, to determine if community needs are being met by these programs, to define the role of program supervisors, and to evaluate if existing roles of program supervisors readily allowed the department to meet the program needs of the community.

Taylor, Gordon D. *Techniques in the Evaluation of Recreational Use.* Ottawa, Canada, Department of Indian Affairs and Northern Development, 1968. Originally a paper presented for the Ninth Commonwealth Forestry Conference, this report proposes planning and data collection techniques for evaluating recreational use as an integral part of the decision-making and policy-making processes.

Theobald, William F. *The Female in Public Recreation: A Study of Participation and Administrative Attitudes.* Vanier City, Ontario, Canadian Park and Recreation Association, 1976. An analysis of female participation in municipal recreation programs, this study assesses participation patterns, employment practices, program integration, resource allocation, printed materials, and administrative attitudes toward females in general, females as participants, and females as staff members. Methodology included structured interviews, questionnaires, observation, and analysis of printed materials.

Urban Institute and International City Management Association. *Measuring the Effectiveness of Basic Municipal Services: Initial Report.* Washington, D.C., The Institute and The Association, February 1974. This report identifies an interim list of measures of service effectiveness—that is, service quality of selected municipal services (including recreation)—and provides preliminary suggestions on data collection procedures. Specific measures include program effectiveness, efficiency, and workload performance.

U.S. Department of Housing and Urban Development. *A Guide for Local Evaluation.* Washington, D.C., U.S. Government Printing Office, 1976. A series of papers presented at a three-day seminar sponsored by HUD's Office of Evaluation that concern the techniques of local evaluation studies such as objectives, criteria, data collection, processing, and report preparation.

van der Smissen, Betty. *Evaluation and Self-Study of Public Recreation and Park Agencies: A Guide with Standards and Evaluative Criteria.* Arlington, Virginia, National Recreation and Park Association, 1972. An evaluation guide to public recreation and park agencies with respect to its philosophy and goals, administration, programming, personnel, evaluation, areas, facilities, and equipment. Standards and evaluative criteria are proposed for each category and subcategory and a formula is proposed to help individual departments assess the degree to which they are in compliance with recommended minimum standards.

Waller, John D., et al. *Monitoring for Government Agencies.* Washington, D.C., The Urban Institute, February 1976. This document identifies the major tasks involved in overcoming the problems associated with gathering information on program effectiveness, and presents procedures that can be utilized to establish an effective monitoring system for a diverse set of projects.

Williams, John G. and C. R. Edginton. "Tuning Up for High Performance," *Parks and Recreation.* Vol. 12, No. 10, October 1977, pp. 36–40, 45. The article describes a total performance measurement system used in the Sunnyvale, California, Department of Parks and Recreation. One element of the system is to provide feedback by continuous performance evaluation of services. Principle data-gathering tools are surveys of citizen satisfaction and employee attitudes. Management By Objectives (MBO) technique and computerized budget information are also incorporated.

Willoughby, Joyce E. "Evaluating Park and Recreation Programs," *Profile.* No. 2, 1976. Terre Haute, Indiana, Indiana Park and Recreation Association, Summer 1976. pp. 8–9. This article deals with recreation program evaluation, and a proposal for a criterion-referenced approach to evaluating therapuetic recreation is offered as an alternative to norm-referenced evaluation approaches.

Wolfensberger, Wolf and Linda Glenn. *PASS: Program Analysis of Service Systems.* Toronto, National Institute on Mental Retardation, York University Campus, 1973. This two-monograph series, composed of a handbook and a field manual, describes a method for the quantitative evaluation of human services. The method rates a service project on 41 major characteristics, then groups the ratings into clusters in order to assess qualitative aspects of service. An optional part of PASS called FUNDET (funding determination) can be utilized to determine funding priorities of service programs where important parts other than service quality must play a part in decision making.

Zuzanek, Jiri. *The Determinants of Leisure Demand and the Prospects for Leisure.* Ottawa, Canada, Leisure Products and Crafts Division, Industry, Trade, and Commerce, May 1976. The report provides industry and government officials with the overall framework required both to properly assess market opportunities in the leisure industry and to develop a plan of action to maximize its contribution to Canada's economic and social objectives. The concept of leisure as it relates to marketable goods and services, the identification of economic and social developments likely to influence leisure spending, and a determination of the leisure market future growth prospects are analyzed.

BIBLIOGRAPHY

Abert, James G., and Murray Kamrass, eds. *Social Experiments and Social Program Evaluation*. Cambridge, Mass.: Ballinger Publishing Co., 1974.

American Association for Health, Physical Education, and Recreation. *Recreation Research*. Washington, D.C.: The Association, 1966.

American Institute for Research. *Evaluative Research Strategies and Methods*. Pittsburgh, Pa.: The Institute, 1970.

American Park and Outdoor Art Association. "Report of Park Census for 1901." *Park and Cemetery and Landscape Gardening* **11** (August 1901). pp. 37–40.

Anderson, Jackson M. "Evaluating Community Recreation." *Journal of the American Association for Health, Physical Education, and Recreation* **24**:5 (May 1953), pp. 25–26, 42.

Armstrong, R. J., T. Cornell, R. E. Kramer, and E. W. Roberson. *The Development and Evaluation of Behavioral Objectives*. Worthington, Ohio: Charles A. Jones Publishing Co., 1970.

Avedon, Elliott M. *Therapeutic Recreation Service: An Applied Behavioral Science Approach*. Englewood Cliffs, N.J.: Prentice-Hall, 1974.

Bannon, Joseph J. *Leisure Resources: Its Comprehensive Planning*. Englewood Cliffs, N.J.: Prentice-Hall, 1976.

Barnsby, S. *Cost-Benefit Analysis and Manpower Programs*. Lexington, Mass.: D.C. Heath Co., 1972.

Bateman, Worth. "Assessing Program Effectiveness: A Rating System for Identifying Relative Program Success." *Welfare in Review* **6**:1 (January 1968), pp. 1–10.

Berelson, Bernard, and Gary Steiner. *Human Behavior: An Inventory of Scientific Findings*. New York: Harcourt, Brace, and World, 1964.

Bernstein, Ilene, ed. *Sociological Methods and Research: Special Issue on Validity Issues in Evaluative Research* **4**:1 (August 1975). Beverly Hills, Cal.: Sage Publications.

Bernstein, Ilene, and Howard E. Freeman. *Academic and Entrepreneurial Research: The Consequences of Diversity in Federal Evaluation Studies*. New York: Russell Sage Foundation, 1975.

Berryman, Doris. *Recommended Standards with Evaluative Criteria for Recreation Services in Residential Institutions*. New York: New York University, School of Education, 1971.

Bigman, Stanley K. "Evaluation Research Review." *Journal of Leisure Research* **1**:2 (Spring 1969), pp. 209–11.

————. "Evaluating the Effectiveness of Religious Programs." *Review of Religious Research* 2 (Winter 1961).

Brown, Robert, and Donald Fisk. *Recreation Planning and Analysis in Local Government*. Washington, D.C.: The Urban Institute, June 1973.

Buchanan, Garth, and Joseph Wholey. "Federal Level Evaluation." *Evaluation* 1:1 (1972), pp. 17–22.

Bureau of Outdoor Recreation, U.S. Department of the Interior. *How Effective are Your Community Recreation Services?* Washington, D.C.: U.S. Government Printing Office, April 1973.

————. *Outdoor Recreation: A Legacy for America*. Washington, D.C.: U.S. Government Printing Office, 1973.

Bureau of Recreation, State of Wisconsin. *Recreation Site Evaluation: Development Series*. Madison, Wis.: The Bureau, 1968.

Butler, George. *Introduction to Community Recreation*, 5th ed. New York: McGraw-Hill, 1976.

Campbell, Donald T. "Reformers as Experiments." Struening, Elmer L. and Marcia Guttentag, eds. *Handbook of Evaluation Research*, vol. 1. Beverly Hills, Cal.: Sage Publications, 1975.

Canadian Treasury Board. *Planning, Programming, Budgeting Guide*. Ottawa: The Queen's Printer, 1969.

Caro, Francis G., ed. *Readings in Evaluation Research*. New York: Russell Sage Foundation, 1971.

————. "Issues in the Evaluation of Social Programs." *Review of Educational Research* 41:2 (1971), pp. 87–114.

————. "Approach to Evaluation Research: A Review." *Human Organization* 28:2 (1969), pp. 87–99.

Carter, Novia, and Brian Wharf. *Evaluating Social Development Programs*. Ottawa: The Canadian Council on Social Development, 1973.

Cherney, Paul R., ed. *Making Evaluation Research Useful*. Columbia, Md: American City Corporation, 1971.

Churchman, C. West, Russell L. Ackoff, and Leonard Arnoff. *Introduction to Operations Research*. New York: John Wiley and Sons, 1957.

City of New York, Community Renewal Program. *Recreation Facilities in New York City: A Method of Assigning Budgetary Priorities*. New York: City Planning Commission, November 1968.

Community Council of Greater New York, Research Department. *Comparative Recreation Needs and Services in New York Neighborhoods*. New York: The Council, 1963.

Council on Accreditation. *Standards and Evaluative Criteria for Recreation, Leisure Services and Resources: Curricula Baccalaureate and Masters Degree Programs*. Arlington, Va.: National Recreation and Park Association, 1975.

Davis, Howard R. "Four Ways to Goal Attainment: An Overview."
   Evaluation **1**:2 (1973), pp. 43–49.
De Shane, J. David K. "From My Corner It's Obvious: Programs Need
   Evaluation." *Recreation Canada* **21**:1 (February 1973), p. 3.
Determinants (The) of Demand and the Prospects for Leisure. Ottawa:
   Industry, Trade and Commerce, May 1976.
Division of Municipal Recreation and Adult Education. *A Handbook of
   Information: Program Evaluation.* Milwaukee, Milwaukee Public
   Schools, n.d. Mimeographed.
Dolbeare, Kenneth M., ed. *Public Policy Evaluation,* vol. II. Sage Year-
   books in Politics and Public Policy. Beverly Hills, Cal.: Sage Publi-
   cations, 1975.
Dubois, Phillip H., and E. Douglas Mayer, eds. *Research Strategies for
   Evaluating Training.* AERA (American Educational Research Associa-
   tion) Monograph Series on Curriculum Evaluation, No. 4. Chicago:
   Rand McNally and Co., 1971.
Dulles, Foster Rhea. A History of Recreation: *America Learns to Play,*
   2nd ed. New York, Appleton-Century Co., 1965.
Dunn, Diana, and Harry Hatry. *Measuring the Effectiveness of Local
   Government Services—Recreation.* Washington, D.C.: The Urban
   Institute, 1971.
Economic Analysis Unit. "How Americans Pursue Happiness." *U.S.
   News and World Report.* **82**:20 (May 23, 1977), pp. 60–76.
————. "83 Billion Dollars for Leisure—Now the Fastest-Growing Busi-
   ness in America." U.S. *News and World Report* **67**:11 (September
   15, 1969), pp. 58–61.
Epstein, Irwin, and Tony Tripodi. *Research Techniques for Program
   Planning, Monitoring and Evaluation.* New York: Columbia Univer-
   sity Press, 1977.
Filkin (Anderson), Kathryn. "A Study of Current Evaluation Practices
   of Major Municipal Recreation Programmes in Ontario." B.A. Project. Waterloo, Ontario, University of Waterloo, June 1976. Type-
   written.
Fischer, Constance T. "Contextual Approach to Assessment." *Com-
   munity Mental Health Journal* **9**:1 (1973), pp. 38–45.
Franklin, Jack L., and Jean H. Thrasher. *An Introduction to Program
   Evaluation.* New York: John Wiley and Sons, 1976.
Gold, Seymour M. "Goals That Count." *Parks and Recreation* **9**:1 (Jan-
   uary 1974), pp. 38, 60–65.
Greenberg, Bernard G., and Berweyn F. Mattison. "The Whys and
   Wherefores of Program Evaluation." *Canadian Journal of Public
   Health* **46**:7 (1955), pp. 293–99.
Great Lakes District Program Standards Committee. *Evaluation of Com-*

munity Recreation: A Guide to Evaluation with Standards and Evaluative Criteria. New York: National Recreation Association, 1965.

Gronlund, Norman E. *Stating Behavioral Objectives for Classroom Instruction.* New York: MacMillan Co., 1970.

Gunn, C. A., and A. J. Worms. *Evaluating and Developing Tourism.* College Station, Texas, Agricultural Experiment Station, Texas A & M University, July 1973.

Hagen, Elizabeth P., and Robert L. Thorndike. "Evaluation." *Encyclopedia of Educational Research,* 3rd ed. New York: The MacMillan Company, 1960, pp. 482–86.

Hatry, Harry, Louis Blair, Donald Fisk, and Wayne Kimmell. *Program Analysis for State and Local Governments.* Washington, D.C.: The Urban Institute, 1976.

Hatry, Harry, P. R. E. Winnie, and D. M. Fish. *Practical Program Evaluation for State and Local Government Officials.* Washington, D.C.: The Urban Institute, 1973.

Herzog, Elizabeth. *Some Guide Lines for Evaluation Research.* Washington, D.C.: Children's Bureau, U.S. Department of Health, Education and Welfare, Social and Rehabilitation Service, 1959.

Holmes, Basil. "Open Spaces, Gardens and Recreation Grounds." *Transactions of the Town Planning Conference, October 1910.* London: The Conference, 1911. pp. 478–493.

Hubbard, Henry V. *The Size and Distribution of Playgrounds and Similar Recreation.* n.p., National Conference on City Planning, August 1914.

Hyman, Herbert H., Charles R. Wright, and Terrance K. Hopkins. *Application of Methods of Evaluation: Four Studies of The Encampment for Citizenship.* Los Angeles: University of California Press, 1962.

Isaac, Stephen, and William B. Michael. *Handbook in Research and Evaluation.* San Diego: Robert R. Knapp, Publishers, 1971.

Johnson, George E. "Play Space for Elementary School Children." *The Playground* 20 (October 1926). pp. 31–35.

Kaufman, Roger. *Needs Assessment.* East Lansing, Mich.: University Consortium for Instructional Development and Technology, 1976.

Kerlinger, Fred N. *Foundations of Behavioral Research,* 4th ed. New York: Holt, Rinehart and Winston, 1973.

Knutson, Andre L. "Evaluation for What?" *Proceedings of the Regional Institute on Neurologically Handicapping Conditions in Children.* Berkeley, Cal.: University of California, June 18–23, 1961.

Koontz, Harold, and C. O'Donnell. *Principles of Management,* 4th ed. New York: McGraw-Hill Book Co., 1968.

Kranthwohl, Daniel R., Benjamin S. Bloom, and B. B. Massia. *Taxon-*

omy of Behavioral Objectives: Handbook II: Affective Domain. New York: David McKay, 1964.

Kraus, Richard G., and Barbara Bates. *Recreation Leadership and Supervision: Guidelines for Professional Development.* Philadelphia: W. B. Saunders Co., 1975.

Lacthau, M., and C. Brown. *The Evaluation Process in Health Education and Recreation.* Englewood Cliffs, N.J., Prentice-Hall, 1962.

Levine, R. A., and A. P. Williams Jr. *Making Evaluation Effective: A Guide.* Santa Monica: Rand Corporation, May 1971.

Livingston, John Leslie, and Sanford C. Gunn. *Accounting for Social Goals: Budgeting and Analysis of Nonmarket Projects.* New York: Harper and Row, 1974.

London, Board of Education. *The Playground Movement in America and Its Relation to Public Education.* Educational Pamphlet No. 27. London, His Majesty's Stationery Office, 1913.

————. *Report of the Departmental Committee Appointed to Inquiry into Certain Questions in Connexion with the Playgrounds of Public Elementary Schools with Abstracts of Evidence.* London, His Majesty's Stationery Office, 1912.

Lutzin, Sidney G., and Edward H. Storey, eds. *Managing Municipal Leisure Services.* Washington, D.C.: International City Management Association, 1973.

Lyden, F. J. *Planning, Programming, Budgeting: A Systems Approach to Management.* Chicago, Markham Publishing Co., 1968.

Mager, Robert F. *Preparing Instructional Objectives,* 2nd ed. Palo Alto, Cal.:, Fearon Publishers, 1975.

Mannell, Roger C. "Evaluation Resources for Recreation Programs." Workshop Report. Wolfeville, Nova Scotia, Acadia University, Center of Leisure Studies, 1977. Mimeographed.

McDill, Edward L., Mary S. McDill, and J. Tillman Sprehe. *Strategies for Success in Compensatory Education: An Appraisal of Evaluation Research.* Baltimore, Johns Hopkins Press, 1969.

McLean, Christine, and Charles R. Spears. "Leisure Programs: Quandary or Quality." *Parks and Recreation* **10**:7 (July 1975), pp. 21–23, 42–45.

Meserow, L. Hale, David T. Pompel Jr., and Charles M. Reich. "Benefit-Cost Evaluation." *Parks and Recreation* **10**:2 (February 1975), pp. 29–30, 40.

Middle Atlantic District Advisory Committee. *A Guide for the Evaluation of Community Recreation.* New York: National Recreation Association, n.d.

Morris, L. N. *Critical Path Analysis.* Oxford, England: Pergamon Press, 1967.

Moursund, Janet P. *Evaluation: An Introduction to Research Design.* Monterey, Cal.: Brooks/Cole Publishing Co., 1973.

Nasatir, D. "Social Science Data Libraries." *American Sociologist* 2 (1967), pp. 78–79.

Nash, Jay B. *The Organization and Administration of Playgrounds and Recreation.* New York: A. S. Barnes and Co., 1927.

National Council of YMCAs of Canada. *Effective Program Planning and Basic Program Evaluation Criteria.* Toronto, The Council, July 1973.

National Recreation Association. *Schedule for the Appraisal of Community Recreation.* New York: The Association, 1951.

———. "Play Space for Schools." New York: The Association, November 1938. Mimeographed.

———. "Types of Municpal Recreation Areas," *The Playground.* 30 (March 1937), pp. 26–31.

National Recreation and Park Association. *Outdoor Recreation Space Standards.* Washington, D.C.: The Association, 1965.

National Science Foundation. Reviews of Data on Research and Development, No. 17. Washington, D.C.: The Foundation, 1960.

Nienaber, Jeanne, and Aaron Wildavsky. *The Budgeting and Evaluation of Federal Recreation Programs or, Money Doesn't Grow on Trees.* New York: Basic Books, 1973.

Office of Education, U.S. Department of Health, Education and Welfare. *Preparing Evaluation Reports: A Guide for Authors.* Washington, D.C.: U.S. Government Printing Office, 1970.

Pierce, Charles H. "Program Evaluation: Future Perspectives." *Recreation Canada* 30:2 (April 1972), pp. 24–30, 35.

Poland, Orville. "Program Evaluation." *Public Administration Review* 34 (July–August 1974), pp. 299–330.

Popham, W. James. *Evaluation in Education: Current Applications.* Berkeley, Cal.:, McCutchan Publishing Corp., 1974.

Provus, Malcolm. *Discrepancy Evaluation.* Berkeley, Cal., McCutchan Publishing Corp., 1971.

Rath, Clovia, and Gustave J. Rath. "Evaluation Is a Process: Systems Analysis in Education." *Educational Technology* March, 1973), pp. 60–62.

Recreation and Youth Services Planning Council of Los Angeles. "An Instrument for Determining Comparative Priority of Need for Neighborhood Recreation Services in the City of Los Angeles." Los Angeles, Cal., The Council, September 1968. Mimeographed.

———. *A Behavioral Approach to Evaluating the Effectiveness of Recreation and Youth Services Programs.* Los Angeles: The Council, September 1966.

Rehabilitation Services Administration, U.S. Department of Health,

Education and Welfare. *Program Evaluation: A Beginning Statement.* Washington, D.C.: U.S. Government Printing Office, 1972.

Rivlin, Alice M. *Systematic Thinking for Social Action.* Washington, D.C.: The Brookings Institution, 1971.

Rossi, Peter H., and Walter Williams. *Evaluating Social Action Programs: Theory, Practice, and Politics.* New York: Seminar Press, 1972.

Salasin, Susan. "Setting Program Priorities for People: Evaluating Environmental Programs." *Evaluation* **1**:3 (1973), pp. 14–16.

Sapora, Allen V. "Evaluation of Park and Recreation Operations: Who Should Do It?" *Parks and Recreation* **4**:12 (December 1969), pp. 35–36, 50–51.

Schulberg, Herbert C., Alan Sheldon, and Frank Baker. *Program Evaluation in the Health Fields.* New York: Behavioral Publications, 1970.

Schulberg, Herbert C., and Frank Baker. "Program Evaluation Models and the Implementation of Research Findings." *American Journal of Public Health* **58**:7 (July 1968), pp. 44–52.

Scriven, Michael. "The Methodology of Evaluation." Tyler, Ralph W., Robert M. Gagne, and Michael Scriven, eds. *Perspectives of Curriculum Evaluation.* AERA Monograph Series on Curriculum Evaluation, No. 1. Chicago: Rand McNally and Co., 1967, pp. 39–83.

Sessoms, H. Douglas. "Education for Recreation and Park Professions," *Parks and Recreation* **2**:12 (December 1967), pp. 29–30, 51.

Sewell, W. R. D., John Davis, A. D. Scott, and D. W. Ross. *Guide to Benefit-Cost Analysis.* Resources for Tomorrow Conference. Ottawa, Information Canada, 1965.

Smith, Stephen, Richard Nuxoll, and Fred Galloway. *Survey Research for Community Recreation Services.* Research Report 291. East Lansing, Mich.: Agricultural Experiment Station, Michigan State University, February 1976.

Stake, Robert E. "The Countenance of Educational Evaluation." *Teachers College Record* **68**:7 (1967), pp. 523–40.

————. *Evaluating Educational Programs: The Need and the Response.* Paris: Organization for Economic Cooperation and Development, 1976.

Stein, Thomas A. *SPRE Report on the State of Recreation and Park Education in Canada and the United States.* Arlington, Va.: National Recreation and Park Association, October 1975.

Stein, Thomas A., and Roger A. Landcaster. "Professional Preparation." *Parks and Recreation* **11**:7 (July 1976), pp. 54–66.

Steiner, Jesse F. *Americans at Play.* New York: McGraw-Hill, 1933.

Struening, Elmer L., and Marcia Guttentag, eds. *Handbook of Evaluation Research,* 2 vols. Beverly Hills, Cal.: Sage Publications, 1975.

Stufflebeam, Daniel L., Walter J. Foley, William J. Gephart, Egon G. Guba, Robert I. Hammond, Howard O. Merriman, and Malcomb M. Provus. *Educational Evaluation and Decision Making.* Itasca, Ill.: F. E. Peacock Publishers, 1971.

Stufflebeam, Daniel L. "Self-Study of Approaches to Evaluation." Popham, W. James, ed. *Evaluation in Education: Current Approaches.* Berkeley, Cal., McCutchan Publishing Corp., 1974.

Suchman, Edward A. "Evaluating Educational Programs: A Symposium." *Urban Review* **3**:4 (1969), pp. 14–22.

————. *Evaluation Research: Principles and Practices in Public Service and Action Programs.* New York: Russell Sage Foundation, 1967.

Taylor, Gordon D. *Techniques in the Evaluation of Recreational Use.* Ottawa: National Parks Canada, 1968.

Theobald, William F. *The Female in Public Recreation: A Study of Participation and Administrative Attitudes.* Vanier City, Ontario: Canadian Park and Recreation Association, 1976.

Timenes, Nicolai Jr. "Recreation." Abert, James G., and Murray Kamrass, eds. *Social Experiments and Social Program Evaluation.* Cambridge, Mass.: Ballinger Publishing Co., 1974, pp. 79–94.

Toffler, Alvin. *Future Shock.* New York: Bantam Books, 1970.

Treischl, M. Fred. "Some Dimensions of Leadership Evaluation in a Children's Activity Programme". *Recreation Review* 2:4 (November 1972), pp. 16–20.

Tripodi, Tony, Phillip Fellin, and Irwin Epstein. *Social Program Evaluation: Guidelines for Health, Education and Welfare Administrators.* Itasca, Ill.: F. E. Peacock Publishers, 1971.

Unkel, M. B., A. W. Smith, and C. S. Van Doren. "Putting Computers to Good Use." *Parks and Recreation* **10**:11 (November 1975), pp. 19–20, 35–37.

Urban Institute and International City Management Association. *Measuring the Effectiveness of Basic Municipal Services: Initial Report.* Washington, D.C.: The Institute and The Association, February 1974.

van der Smissen, Betty. *Evaluation and Self-Study of Public Recreation and Park Agencies: A Guide with Standards and Evaluative Criteria.* Washington, D.C.: National Recreation and Park Association, 1972.

Waller, John D., Dona MacNeil Kemp, John W. Scanlon, Francine Tolson, and Joseph S. Wholey. *Monitoring for Governmental Agencies.* Washington, D.C.: The Urban Institute, February 1976.

Warheit, George, Roger A. Bell, and John S. Schwab. *Planning for Change: Needs Assessment Approaches.* Washington, D.C.: National Institute of Mental Health, n.d.

Watters, Thomas. "The Leisure-Time Market and Its Impact on the

Economy of Our Country." *Recreation Management* **16**:10 (December 1973), pp. 48–51.

Weiss, Carol H., and Harry P. Hatry. *An Introduction to Sample Surveys for Governmental Managers.* Washington, D.C.: The Urban Institute, March 1971.

Weiss, Carol H., ed. *Evaluating Action Programs: Readings in Social Action and Education.* Boston: Allyn and Bacon, 1972.

———. *Evaluation Research: Methods of Assessing Program Effectiveness.* Englewood Cliffs, N.J.: Prentice-Hall, 1972.

Wholey, Joseph S., John W. Scanlon, Hugh G. Duffy, James S. Fukumoto, and Leona M. Vogt. *Federal Evaluation Policy.* Washington, D.C.: The Urban Institute, 1970.

Wilder, Robert L. "EEI: A Survival Tool." *Parks and Recreation* **12**:8 (August 1977), pp. 22–24, 50–51.

Willer, Barry, Gary H. Miller, and Lucie Cantrell, eds. *Information and Feedback for Evaluation.* Toronto: York University, Communications Department, November 1975.

Wolfensberger, Wolf, and Linda Glenn. *Pass: Program Analysis of Service Systems: A Method for the Quantitative Evaluation of Human Services.* Handbook and Field Manual. Downsview, Ontario: National Institute on Mental Retardation, 1973.

Worthen, Blaine R., and James R. Sanders. *Educational Evaluation: Theory and Practice.* Worthington, Ohio: Charles A. Jones Publishing Co., 1973.

Youth and Recreation Branch. *Evaluation: Notes for Community Leaders,* No. 9. Toronto: Ontario Ministry of Community and Social Services, n.d. Mimeographed.

———. *Municipal Recreation Bulletin 11:* Evaluation. Toronto: Ontario Ministry of Community and Social Services, n.d. Mimeographed.

AUTHOR INDEX

SUBJECT INDEX